HOW TO GUIDE
GIRL SCOUT BROWNIES THROUGH

A WORLD OF GIRLS

IT'S YOUR STORY—TELL IT! *A LEADERSHIP JOURNEY*

Girl Scouts of the USA

girl scouts

CHAIR,
NATIONAL BOARD
OF DIRECTORS
Connie L. Lindsey

CHIEF
EXECUTIVE
OFFICER
Kathy Cloninger

CHIEF OPERATING
OFFICER
Jan Verhage

VICE PRESIDENT,
PROGRAM
Eileen Doyle

WRITTEN BY Jane Smalley, Andrea Bastiani Archibald,
Valerie Takahama, and Laura J. Tuchman
PROJECT EDITOR: Frankie Wright
EXECUTIVE EDITOR, JOURNEYS: Laura J. Tuchman
ILLUSTRATED BY Helena Garcia
DESIGNED BY Emily Peterson
PROGRAM TEAM: Douglas Bantz, Ellen Kelliher,
Sarah Micklem, Sheryl O'Connell, Lesley Williams
DIRECTOR, PROGRAM RESOURCES: Suzanne Harper

© 2010 by Girl Scouts of the USA

First published in 2010 by Girl Scouts of the USA
420 Fifth Avenue, New York, NY 10018-2798
www.girlscouts.org

ISBN: 978-0-88441-756-9

Printed in Italy

4 5 6 7 8 9/17 16 15 14 13 12 11

PHOTOGRAPHS: Page 8: Lesley Williams; Page 60: Makiko Hoh

the dove
self-esteem
fund

This publication was made
possible by a generous grant
from the Dove Self-Esteem Fund.

Mixed Sources
Product group from well-managed
forests and other controlled sources
www.fsc.org   Cert no. SQS-COC-100209
© 1996 Forest Stewardship Council
FSC

Text printed on Fedrigoni Cento
Certified mixed sources.
Covers printed on Prisma artboard
FSC Certified mixed sources.

CONTENTS

Building girls' **confidence**

is the goal of this *It's Your Story—Tell It!* journey.

Building confidence every day.

Girl Scouting builds girls of **courage, confidence, and character,** who make the world a better place.

That's our **mission.** And we do it through 3 keys to leadership: **Discover + Connect + Take Action**

On this journey...

Girl Scout Brownies learn to use clues in stories to make the world better.

Then they get creative—through a medium of their choice—and tell their story of what they accomplished.

Finding clues to better the world and sharing stories of their success—that builds confidence!

Imagine how far a Brownie can go and how much she can do—for herself *and* the world—when she has confidence.

Now, multiply that confidence by 720,000, the number of Girl Scout Brownies in the world. These Brownies will be leaders in their own lives and leaders in the world—because they Discover, Connect, and Take Action. That's a future to journey toward!

What to pack for the journey!

Girl Scout leadership journeys invite girls to explore a theme through many experiences and from many perspectives— through the 3 keys to leadership: **Discover + Connect + Take Action**

All the joys of travel are built right in! So fill your suitcase with everything you need for an amazing trip that will change girls' lives!

The Girls' Book

Engaging stories, fun activities, recipes, and creative projects let girls . . . meet new people, explore new things, make memories, gather keepsakes, and earn badges— all while exploring a theme through the 3 keys to leadership!

The Adult Guide

Easy activities to get girls thinking and doing while team-building, being creative, and boosting their sense of self—as they explore the 3 keys to leadership! Plus: healthful snacks, and loads of tips for engaging girls in leadership.

Your Wider Community

Reach out to local experts on . . . storytelling and the arts. And to local partners: libraries, booksellers, and arts groups.

Your Enthusiasm

And your creativity, your partnership with girls and families, and, most important, your willingness to learn by doing, right alongside the girls!

Stories + Their Clues = A Fun Way to Build Girls' Confidence as Leaders

This Girl Scout leadership journey is part of a series that invites girls into the fun and friendly world of storytelling.

Stories are fundamental to how girls learn about themselves and the world.

Stories allow girls to absorb the ideas and richness of many cultures, and that develops their empathy, tolerance, and acceptance of others.

Stories sharpen girls' minds and spark their imaginations.

Stories inspire and motivate.

Stories teach girls how to lead and keep them growing as leaders.

Stories and Clues Are Everywhere! Stories are all around us—in ads, memoir projects, TV shows, in magazines, on the news, and even on cereal boxes! From the beginning of this journey to the end, the Brownies are engaged in the world of stories in a way that gets them looking for clues to make the world better.

Stories about fictional girls

The girls' book has three inviting stories full of fun and clues:

"Flying into Shali's Desert Home"

"Dancing with Chosita"

"Story Swapping with Lakti"

Inspiring stories about real girls and women

who have found clues and made the world better!

A book for every girl!

So that girls can enjoy the journey whenever they like, it's important that each girl has her own journey book. They can draw inspiration from the book and add their personal inspirations to it! This book may become their own journey journal—and one of the many mementos the girls will cherish throughout their years in Girl Scouting and beyond!

How Brownies Find Clues!

The Brownies find clues in stories by asking themselves:

What could be made better for the girl or girls in this story, and is this something I can make better in my community, too?

Thousands of stories about girls hold great clues for the Brownies. The examples here span a range of reading levels and will appeal to younger and older Brownies. You might check with librarians and booksellers, too, if you want more examples. The girls may have their own favorites to add. Also, check out the chart on page 47 to see how story clues can unfold into a project for change along the journey.

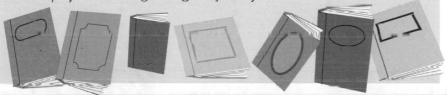

Princesses who offer clues!

With royalty sprinkled through this journey, the Brownies might enjoy these princess tales with clues:

Cinder Edna
by Ellen Jackson

Princess Smartypants
by Babette Cole

Princess Grace
by Mary Hoffman

The King's Equal
by Katherine Paterson

The Paper Bag Princess
by Robert Munsch

STORIES TO SHARE

NONFICTION

Game Face: What Does a Female Athlete Look Like by Jane Gottesman. First-hand accounts of athletes and their achievements.

Girls Think of Everything: Stories of Ingenious Inventions by Women by Catherine Thimmesh.

Girls Who Looked Under Rocks: The Lives of Six Pioneering Naturalists by Jeannine Atkins. Girls who became notable scientists.

The Sky's the Limit: Stories of Discovery by Women and Girls by Catherine Thimmesh.

FICTION

Amelia's Road by Linda Jacobs Altman. Traveling with her crop-picking family, Amelia creates a place all her own.

Because of Winn-Dixie, novel and film by Kate DiCamillo. In a new town, a girl makes friends through her dog.

The Garden of Happiness by Erika Tamar. Marisol contributes to a community garden in her neighborhood.

The Great Gilly Hopkins by Katherine Paterson. Gilly, a foster child, wants a place to call home.

The Hundred Dresses by Eleanor Estes. Wanda copes with poverty and teasing.

The Lotus Seed by Sherry Garland. A girl shares the story of her grandmother coming from Vietnam to America.

Love from Your Friend, Hannah by Mindy Warshaw Skolsky. A girl copes with adults losing jobs during the Depression.

Mama, Do You Love Me? by Barbara M. Joosse. An Inuit girl finds love in the details of her life.

Miss Rumphius by Barbara Cooney. Miss Rumphius lives a life that leaves the world more beautiful.

My Name Is Yoon by Helen Recorvits. A Korean girl is true to herself in a new land.

The Recess Queen by Alexis O'Neill. Katie Sue takes care of a school bully, Mean Jean.

Roxaboxen by Alice McLerran. Marian and friends create an entire town to play in.

Yours Turly, Shirley by Ann M. Martin. Shirley has trouble reading but finds her own strengths.

Why Self-Esteem Matters!

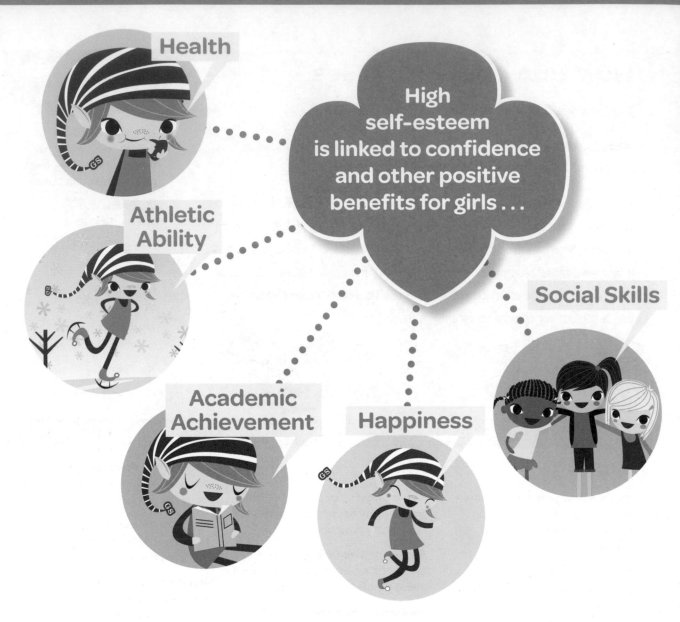

Health

Athletic Ability

High self-esteem is linked to confidence and other positive benefits for girls . . .

Social Skills

Academic Achievement

Happiness

Self-esteem means how a girl feels about herself—her abilities, her body, her capacity to seek and meet challenges in the world. On average, the self-esteem of Brownie-age girls is relatively high, and keeping that self-esteem high is one of the goals of this journey. That way, as the girls grow, they're more likely to avoid the drop in self-esteem that is so typical in adolescence. Without that drop, their confidence can soar!

Session Plans Make the Most of Brownies' Skills

The Sample Session plans starting on page 28 offer opportunities for the girls to enhance their skills and develop new ones, while taking into account the abilities and needs of Brownie-age girls. When planning additional creative adventures, keep in mind that second- and third-graders:

have lots of energy and need to run, walk, and play outside.	*So take your session activities outside whenever possible. Girls' creativity might even be further inspired by nature and fresh air!*
enjoy doing things in groups.	*So allow them to team up for art projects and performances.*
want to help, and appreciate being given responsibilities.	*So let girls lead, direct, and help out in activities whenever possible. Allow the group to make decisions about roles and responsibilities.*
are concrete thinkers and focused on the "here and now."	*So ask them questions to gauge their understanding of stories and allow them to role-play their own pretend visit to a new country.*
need clear directions and structure.	*So offer only one direction at a time and, when you can, let the girls know what's coming up next in the get-together or in future gatherings.*
are becoming comfortable with number concepts and time.	*So offer support only when needed—have the girls help create the schedule and flow of their get-togethers, and count out money for trips.*
are developing fine-motor skills and can use basic tools.	*So encourage them to express themselves and their creativity by making things with their hands.*
love to create music and dance.	*So they might like to create a play or tell a story through dance.*
know how to follow rules, listen, and appreciate recognition.	*So acknowledge when the girls have listened or followed the directions well. It will increase their motivation for listening and following again!*

Promoting Well-Being Along the Journey

Girl Scouting is guided by a positive philosophy of inclusion that benefits all. On this journey, especially, it is hoped that girls will increase their feelings of being powerful, capable, and strong as they enhance their skills and develop new ones. So, as the Girl Scout Law says, "be a sister to every Girl Scout." Be sensitive to whether any girls are new to town, have a disability, don't speak English as a first language, or have parents getting a divorce. Often what counts most is being open-minded and aware, staying flexible, and creatively varying your approach with the girls.

Four Leadership Awards

IF A GIRL MISSES AN AWARD STEP . . .

Find a way for her to do something similar to what she missed so she can still earn the award with her group. Your goal is to guide her to have the same learning and growing opportunity—and to understand how she can contribute to the team. You might ask all the Brownies to brainstorm about how girls who miss steps can get back on track with the journey.

Girls may not experience activities in exactly the same way, but they can each take away new insights, connections, and a sense of accomplishment.

Hear a Story Award

What it means for Brownies: They see that stories hold clues for how to better the world.

How Brownies earn it: By finding a clue in a story that represents a change they can make in their world.

When Brownies receive it: Session 2

Change a Story Award

What it means for Brownies: They realize they have the power to change things for the better.

How Brownies earn it: They act on a clue to change things for the better for girls in their world.

When Brownies receive it: Session 7

Tell a Story Award

What it means for Brownies: They have the confidence and knowledge to educate and inspire others.

How Brownies earn it: They teach others about the change they created in their community and inspire their audience to support the change, too.

When Brownies receive it: Session 9

Better World for Girls! Award

What it means for Brownies: They understand that they belong to a large and far-reaching world of girls.

How Brownies earn it: They use creative expression (of their choice) to show what it means to them to be part of a larger world of girls.

When Brownies receive it: Session 10

LADDER OF LEADERSHIP

As Girl Scouts take journeys and earn the awards, they're climbing a ladder that lets them be leaders in their own lives and in the world! Pass it on!

It's Your World— Change It!

It's Your Story— Tell It!

It's Your Planet— Love It!

Ambassadors raise their voices to advocate for issues they care about.

Girls move dreams forward!

Ambassadors learn that leaders aim for justice.

AMBASSADOR

Seniors learn that leaders have a vision and can move the world a step closer to it.

Girls see how much sisterhood does for the world!

Seniors find out what leaders can sow for Earth.

SENIOR

Cadettes develop the people skills that leaders need.

Girls put the ME in media.

Cadettes become leaders in clearing the air!

CADETTE

Juniors learn that leaders need power—their own, their team's, and their community's.

Girls explore all the roles open to them in life.

Juniors bring energy solutions to the world.

JUNIOR

Girls explore their place in the wide world of girls.

Brownies take the lead in saving Earth's water.

Brownies go on a quest to find the three keys to leadership.

BROWNIE

Girls learn they can care for animals and themselves.

Daisies have fun—and learn leadership skills—in the garden.

DAISY

Daisies learn to protect Earth's treasures.

What You'll Find in Each Sample Session Plan

THE JOURNEY SNAPSHOT gives an overview of what's ahead.

JOURNEY SNAPSHOT

SESSION 1 Girls Around the World	The Brownies are introduced to the journey and its awards. They start a Team Passport, play games from around the world, and explore how games and stories link them to a wider world of girls.
SESSION 2 Girls in Our World	The Brownies see how they belong to many circles, or "worlds," of girls, and explore how stories of women and girls often hold clues about actions they can take to make the world better. They earn their Hear a Story Award.
SESSION 3 From Story Clues to Story Change	The Brownies explore how they can use clues to create change in their world, play relay games to create stories, and experience and appreciate diversity in the world.
SESSION 4 Planning for Change a Story	The Brownies begin to make a positive change in the world around them as they start their Change a Story project. They use role-play scenarios to practice communication skills, make and enjoy healthful (lamb) snacks, and get active with a team dance.
SESSIONS 5 & 6 Change a Story: Making It Happen	Brownies team up to carry out their story project. They create self-portraits to express their uniqueness, act out favorite stories in story charades, and explore clues for change in a story about Juliette Gordon Low.
SESSIONS 7 & 8 Planning and Telling Our Story of Change	The Brownies earn their Change a Story Award and then plan for and present their story of change, and inspire their audience to keep that change going. They also explore stories in advertising and media, and create their own ads.
SESSION 9 Our Whole Story	The Brownies consider their place in the world of girls and plan their final journey celebration. They earn their Tell a Story Award, and create a team quilt that expresses their own strengths and tells the story of their Brownie world of girls.
SESSION 10 World of Girls Celebration	The Brownies celebrate their place in the world of girls with their own artistic creations and think about all they've done along the journey. They also say what they want for themselves and the world of girls going forward. They earn their Better World for Girls! Award.

Journey activities are sequenced to give girls lots of fun and exciting challenges centered around earning the journey's three leadership awards. But don't feel you and the girls must do everything in the Sample Sessions or in the order given. Think of journey activities as pieces that can be mixed, matched, and coordinated according to the needs of your group of Brownies.

AT A GLANCE gives the session's goal, activities, and recommended materials.

TOWARD THE AWARD ICONS indicate activities that step girls toward a leadership award.

CEREMONIES, opening and closing, mark the Brownies' time together as special.

SAMPLE SESSION 1
Girls Around the World

AT A GLANCE

A ROUSING BEGINNING

Activities in this session launch the journey's two intertwining themes: the world of girls and the power of stories.

You might set up the session as a special journey kickoff and invite your Friends and Family Network and any Cadettes interested in earning their LiA Award by working with Brownies. That way, everyone starts the journey together!

Crunched for time? Save "Our Globe (or Map) of Girls" for the second gathering. Or simply spread the fun across two sessions—however it suits the girls! You'll know best what will get the Brownies excited about *A World of Girls!*

Goal: The Brownies have fun exploring how stories and games can link them to the wide world of girls—and how they belong to this wide world of girls, too!

- Opening Ceremony: A Circle of Adventure
- Introducing the Journey's Awards
- Team Passport
- Games Around the Globe
- Our Globe (or Map) of Girls
- "Flying into Shali's Desert Home"
- Snack Time: Jordan's Refreshments
- Closing Ceremony: A Great Place!

MATERIALS

- **Team Passport:** paper, markers, and assorted art materials
- **Games Around the Glove:** for *Banyoka,* large objects for obstacles (desks, chairs, books or boxes, traffic cones, large balls); for *Cencio Mollo,* a handkerchief
- **Our Globe (or Map) of Girls:** globe

or world map, sticky notes or slips of paper, tape, yarn, or thread; computer with Internet access (optional, to show the WAGGGS Web site, see page 33)
- **Snack Time:** pita bread, hummus, cut vegetables for dipping; figs or Fig Newtons

PREPARE AHEAD

Talk with any Network members, and Cadettes or other assistants, about their roles for this opening gathering.

Opening Ceremony: A Circle of Adventure

Gather the girls in a circle and welcome them to this journey called *A World of Girls.* You might say something like:

- *Today we're beginning an exciting journey called A World of Girls. You may already know what a journey is. Can anyone tell us? That's right, it's an adventure where you meet new people, see new places, learn new things, and have fun!*
- *On this journey, we'll learn about the lives of girls all over the world. You'll also explore your own world and the girls in it—your families, your friends, and girls from all parts of your life.*
- *How will we do all this? Through stories! We'll hear, read, and talk about stories of women and girls. You'll see that stories have clues in them about how to make the world a better place.*

Then say something like: *Now, let's link arms and imagine that we're forming a circle around the world, and let's say the Girl Scout Promise and the Girl Scout Law together.*

Then start a brief discussion with points like these:

- *We've just said the Girl Scout Promise and the Girl Scout Law, two wonderful things that unite Girl Scouts all around the world. (See inside front cover for the full text of the Promise and Law.) Did you notice how the last line of the Law asks you to "be a sister to every Girl Scout"?*
- *What do you think it means to be "a sister" to all the girls in our Brownie group, and all the Brownies around the world? (If the girls don't answer right away, offer suggestions such as: caring about and learning about one another, having fun together, sharing ideas and feelings.)*

Introducing the Journey's Awards

Let the girls know that on this journey, they'll earn four awards: Hear a Story, Change a Story, Tell a Story, and Better World for Girls! You might point out the pictures of the awards on page 7 of the *GIRLS* side of their book and say: *We'll talk more about these awards as we travel along. For now, let's get started on this fantastic journey!*

IT'S A BIG CIRCLE!

When you add up 720,000 Brownies, plus all the other Girl Scouts, and then all the Girl Guides around the world, the number is in the millions—and counting. That's a wonderfully wide world of girls!

MORE ON AWARDS!

The journey's awards are detailed on page 12 of this guide and on page 7 of the *GIRLS* side of the Brownies' book. You'll have a chance to talk more about them with the Brownies in later sessions.

The steps to earning the awards—and suggested award ceremonies—are built into the journey's Sample Sessions.

Page 7, *GIRLS* side of the Brownies' book

CREATIVE ACTIVITIES
encourage creativity, self-expression, and teamwork.

ACTIVE TIME activities
get girls up and moving!

WHAT TO SAY
A full script for you to use! Must you follow it? No! Let it guide you, but be yourself!

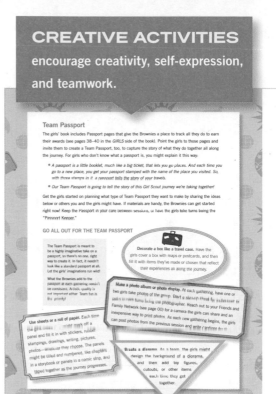

Team Passport

The girls' book includes Passport pages that give the Brownies a place to track all they do to earn their awards (see pages 38–40 in the *GIRLS* side of the book). Point the girls to those pages and invite them to create a Team Passport, too, to capture the story of what they do together all along the journey. For girls who don't know what a passport is, you might explain it this way:

* A passport is a little booklet, much like a big ticket, that lets you go places. And each time you go to a new place, you get your passport stamped with the name of the place you visited. So, with those stamps in it, a passport tells the story of your travels.

* Our Team Passport is going to tell the story of this Girl Scout journey we're taking together!

Get the girls started on planning what type of Team Passport they want to make by sharing the ideas below or others you and the girls might have. If materials are handy, the Brownies can get started right now! Keep the Passport in your care between sessions, or have the girls take turns being the "Passport Keeper."

GO ALL OUT FOR THE TEAM PASSPORT

The Team Passport is meant to be a highly imaginative take on a passport, so there's no one, right way to create it. In fact, it needn't look like a standard passport at all. Let the girls' imaginations run wild!

What the Brownies add to the passport at each gathering needn't be constant. Artistic quality is not important either. Team fun is the priority!

Decorate a box like a travel case. Have the girls cover a box with maps or postcards, and then fill it with items they've made or chosen that reflect their experiences all along the journey.

Use sheets or a roll of paper. Each time the girls meet, ... mark off a panel and fill it in with stickers, rubber stampings, drawings, writing, pictures, photos—whatever they choose. The panels might be titled and numbered, like chapters in a storybook or panels in a comic strip, and taped together as the journey progresses.

Make a photo album or photo display. At each gathering, have one or two girls take photos of the group. Start a sign-up sheet so volunteers or girls can take turns being the photographer. Reach out to your Friends and Family Network (see page 00) for a camera the girls can share and an inexpensive way to print photos. As each new gathering begins, the girls can post photos from the previous session and write captions for it.

Create a diorama. As a team, the girls might design the background of a diorama, and then add toy figures, cutouts, or other items each time they get together.

Games Around the Globe

Next, talk with the girls about games and how much fun they can be. You might say:

* All around the world, girls like to play games, especially games in which they move around.

* Playing games together is a way to get to know others, and active games are important for staying healthy and fit.

* By playing games from around the world, you also get to see what girls in other places like to do.

Then ask the girls to name some games they enjoy and tell what they like about them. After each girl has a chance to share her favorites, invite the group to play *Banyoka* or *Cencio Mollo* (described below) or another game that you know from a country either than your own.

Banyoka, an obstacle course game, can be played indoors or out. Indoor obstacles can include furniture, stacks of books or boxes; outdoor ones can be traffic cones, large balls, or boxes. To play the game:

* Form two teams of equal numbers of girls.

* Each team becomes a "snake": The girls sit on the floor or ground, one behind the other, with their legs open like scissors and their hands on the shoulders, or their arms around the waist, of the girl in front.

* Each team "scootches" along, moving around or over the obstacles while staying connected. The first team to get around its set of obstacles wins.

Variations: The girls form their snake by standing, with arms linked sideways. Or they can act as one team, navigating against the clock through a set of obstacles.

Cencio Mollo: In this traditional Italian game, the girls form a circle and one girl is chosen to be the "It."

* The girl who is "It" stands in the center with a handkerchief and goes to someone in the circle and says, "The *Cencio Mollo* has come to you."

* The girl she is facing says, "Let it come. I shall not cry, laugh, or kiss it." Then the "It" girl tries to make her laugh any way she can, but she can only touch her with the handkerchief on the head or face.

* If the player doesn't laugh, "It" moves on to the next girl in the circle. A player who laughs pays a penalty, such as having to sing a song, jump in the air five times, or do something else silly. Then she becomes "It."

GAMES & STORIES!

Games are like stories! They play out over time with a beginning, a middle, and an end. You might get the girls talking about a game after they play it: First we did this, then this happened and that happened, and then our team won—that's a story!

WHAT'S IN A GAME'S NAME?

Banyoka (pronounced ban yoka) comes from the African countries of Zambia and Zaire, and means "the snake."

Cencio Mollo (pronounced CHEN-cho-MOL-lo) is Italian for wet handkerchief.

SNACKS
offer girls healthful, global-themed energy boosters.

OPTIONS
for fun and learning, and ties to the stories and activities in the Brownies' book.

Jordan's Refreshments

Bring out the hummus and pita bread (along with the cut-up vegetables for dipping), and let the girls know that these are foods eaten in Jordan. If the girls (like the Brownies in the story) have never tasted a fig, have them try one, or a Fig Newton. Get them talking about the cookie's fig "jam" filling and let them know that Fig Newtons were named for the town of Newton, Massachusetts. While they enjoy their snack, they might like to think up treats based on street names, the name of their school, or names of nearby towns.

MORE PASSPORT FUN WITH STORIES!

Before you close, look back with the girls at all the ways they've learned that stories can be told.

Closing Ceremony: A Great Place!

To underscore the global theme of this journey, invite the girls to have some fun reciting a rhyming poem, clapping and reaching out or pointing to one another to match the words they are saying. They can stand together and each say a line from the poem, repeating all lines until everyone has had a turn. Or they can say the remaining lines in unison, and make up their own gestures.

Our journey begins today

... about stories! Ask them to think about girl characters they know from movies, TV shows, books, cartoons, or other sources. Any thoughts they bring back to their next gathering will help with the journey's many story-related activities.

We'll reach even farther
On our adventure to come
As we hear stories about girls
Read stories about girls
And share stories about girls
Like you, and you, and you, and me!
Our world of girls is a great place to be!

Looking Ahead to Session 2

Next time, the girls will seek out clues for their Hear a Story Award. Revisit the award details on page 00 of this guide, along with "Stories + Their Clues" on page 8. Although clues aren't restricted to storybooks, you might plan to meet at a library—a gold mine for stories and clues! Or reach out to your Network to gather a selection of books, magazines, and other story sources to share at your meeting place. Review the lists on page 9 for suggested stories that hold good clues.

OPTIONAL FIELD TRIP TO LIBRARY

To prepare, visit the library on your own and ask if the librarian would lead a discussion with the girls about clues in stories and how to find them. The librarian can likely gather various stories from the library's own collection for the girls to discuss and borrow.

* Share with the librarian the "Stories + Their Clues" section of this guide (page 8) and describe the requirements of the Hear a Story Award (page 12). You might also share a copy of the girls' book.

* Invite the librarian to join with the girls at their final celebration, too, so she can learn all that the Brownies accomplish on the rest of the journey.

OPTIONAL GUEST SPEAKER: A STORY EXPERT

If a library visit isn't an option for your group, invite a librarian, book editor, author, or someone familiar with children's stories to your meeting, to talk with the Brownies about clues in stories, and to inspire them to find more clues on their own.

Pages 8–9, GIRLS side of the Brownies' book.

IMPORTANT LEADERSHIP LESSONS!

As the Brownies move through this journey, they actively engage in things that all leaders do. They . . .

* are on the lookout for ways they can act to help others

* think about the kinds of problems they can help solve in their community.

In upcoming gatherings, the Brownies and you will go on to choose, plan, Take Action, and even educate and inspire others to good changes in the world.

This illustration, from the WORLD side of the Brownies' book, was inspired by the architecture of Amman, Jordan.

Creating a Network of Journey Resources

GIRL SCOUT CADETTES + BROWNIES = MORE FUN!

Girl Scout Cadettes have the opportunity to earn a LiA–a Leader in Action –Award, each time they help Brownies (and you!) along a journey! The LiA requirements for this journey are on pages 18-19.

So, go ahead! Reach out around your Girl Scout community and tag a Cadette or two!

The Brownies will love spending time with cool big sisters. The Cadettes will love this leadership role. And you'll enjoy not having to do everything yourself!

GO ONLINE FOR LETTERS HOME

Visit the Journeys section of girlscouts.org for letters and forms to start your Friends and Family Network, as well as to keep its members informed and motivated to join in the fun! You'll find:

- Welcome Letter

- Sign-Up Form so Network Members can share their skills and expertise

- Take-Home letters for help with journey snacks and art supplies

You'll get a break and expand the girls' awareness of community by asking families, friends, and friends of friends to visit and enhance the Brownies' gatherings. So go ahead and hand off activities and prep steps to a Brownie Friends and Family Network. Here are some tips:

- Before the journey begins, aim for a brief get-together (even online!) with parents, caregivers, relatives, and friends.

- Find out who likes to do what, identify assistants for various activities, and see who has time for behind-the-scenes preparations, gathering supplies (pads, markers, glitter, glue), or snack duty.

- Keep in mind that in some families, an aunt, older sibling, cousin, or other adult may be most able to participate.

More Print and Online Journey Resources

☐ *Girl Scout Safety Activity Checkpoints* detail the safety net provided for girls in Girl Scouting. Seek them out from your council, and keep them handy!

☐ **Journey maps, in the Journeys section of girlscouts.org,** show you and the girls how to mix the outdoors, trips, badges, and Girl Scout traditions (including cookies!) into your journey fun.

☐ *It's Your Journey—Customize It!* is your guide to making the most of Girl Scout leadership journeys.

☐ *Volunteer Essentials* is your guide to all things Girl Scouts! Seek it out from your council.

☐ **Online activities** for girls to enjoy on their own, with friends and with their Brownie group, are at girlscouts.org/itsyourstory.

BROWNIE JOURNEY PEOPLE POWER

FRIENDS & FAMILY NETWORK: Name	Willing to help with:	Phone and e-mail address

GIRL SCOUT CADETTES EARNING LiA: Name	Activities planned:	Phone and e-mail address

COUNCIL CONTACTS: Name	Willing to help with:	Phone and e-mail address

LOCAL EXPERTS: Name	Area of expertise:	Phone and e-mail address

EARNING THE LiA Award

Dear Girl Scout Cadette,

You know how captivating stories can be. Right now, your Brownie sisters are exploring stories about girls—their own stories and stories about girls around the world. The amazing world of girls—that's a page-turner!

You have wonderful stories to tell, too. And if you are now enjoying the *MEdia* journey, you can share another aspect of stories: how media influences girls' stories and how girls can influence the media. So get set to earn the LiA (Leader in Action) Award by using your leadership skills and sharing your media savvy (not to mention your own unique stories) with a team of Brownies in your community.

Here's how:

1. Find a team of Girl Scout Brownies on (or about to begin) their *A World of Girls* journey. Ask the adults who volunteer with your group, or ask your Girl Scout council for tips on how to locate a Brownie team.

2. From their volunteer, find out what the Brownie team is doing. Talk with her about what the Brownies enjoy and what she herself finds challenging. Read the Brownies' *A World of Girls* book and take a look at the adult guide, too.

3. Arrange to be at some of the Brownies' gatherings. Coordinate with the volunteer so you'll have time to do each of these:

☐ Inspire the Brownies to look and listen for stories in their everyday lives. With your knowledge of media, talk about the stories the media creates about girls and how they make girls feel. Together, decide whether media portrayals of girls seem true. Share other stories, too, such as stories of real girls and women you have met or learned about on your Cadette journey.
Date accomplished _____

☐ Guide the Brownies in an activity to develop their teamwork skills. The girls are planning to tell a story together to an audience and create a change in their community. They'll need to work together to make this happen. Maybe you've participated in team-building activities with Cadettes or with other girls in your world. If so, share some tips with the Brownies. If not, get ideas from other Girl Scouts in your area. You might use a team-building activity to open or close a session, or introduce it when it best fits for the Brownie team and its journey.
Date accomplished _____

☐ Inspire the girls to try a healthy new activity, such as a physically active game from another country or culture, or one of your favorite types of exercise or dance. Find ideas in the *A World of Girls* adult guide, or ask the Brownies for some of their favorites. By showing the Brownies the benefits—and fun—of exercise and movement, you'll create a story that features healthy girls of the future.
Date accomplished _____

☐ Encourage the Brownies to use a variety of media and various art forms as they explore storytelling. You might share types of media new to you, or demonstrate a medium in which you have some expertise. Share your interest and knowledge with Brownies as they tell their own stories of who they are and how they are connected to a world of girls.
Date accomplished _____

4. **After you've completed your activities with the Brownies,** ask their volunteer for feedback on what you did. What worked well? What might you change next time?

5. **Now that you've shared stories with the Brownies,** and learned some of their stories, think about and answer these questions:

- In what ways did you **CONNECT** with the younger girls?

- How did your leadership encourage the Brownies to **TAKE ACTION** to create a change in their community?

- What did you **DISCOVER** about yourself as you guided the Brownies?

CONGRATULATIONS! Wear your LiA Award with pride!

Keys to Girl Leadership

Girl Scouting prepares girls to be leaders—in their own daily lives and in the world. We do this through the Girl Scout Leadership Experience, pictured below, which is the basis for everything girls do in Girl Scouting. The three keys to leadership—Discover (self), Connect (team up and network with others), and Take Action (make a difference in the world)—are a shorthand way to capture all of Girl Scouts' 15 national leadership benefits girls receive in Girl Scouting.

As you can see in the charts on pages 102–104, all of the experiences in this journey have been created to engage girls in exploring these three keys to leadership. That's what makes a Girl Scout journey so special: Everything girls and their adult guides need to explore the leadership keys is built right in! So all along the way, you will be guiding the Brownies toward leadership skills and qualities they can use right now—and all their lives. Keep in mind that the intended benefits to girls are the cumulative result of traveling through an entire journey—and everything else girls experience in Girl Scouting!

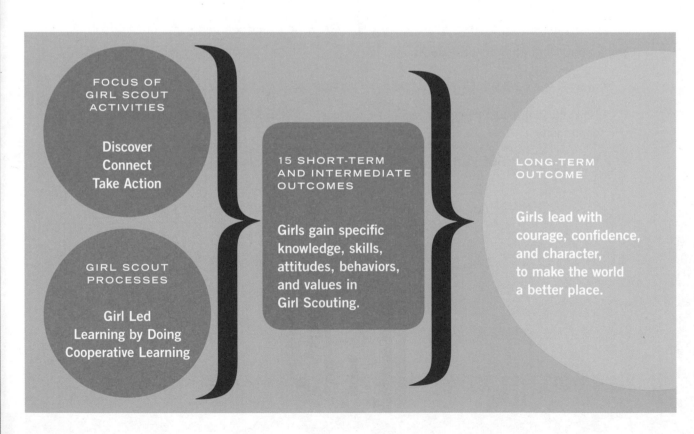

FOCUS OF GIRL SCOUT ACTIVITIES

Discover
Connect
Take Action

GIRL SCOUT PROCESSES

Girl Led
Learning by Doing
Cooperative Learning

15 SHORT-TERM AND INTERMEDIATE OUTCOMES

Girls gain specific knowledge, skills, attitudes, behaviors, and values in Girl Scouting.

LONG-TERM OUTCOME

Girls lead with courage, confidence, and character, to make the world a better place.

How Girls Have Fun in Girl Scouts

In Girl Scouting, girls enjoy activities based on the three keys to leadership and built on three processes that make Girl Scouting unique from school and other extracurricular activities. The keys and processes are written right into the journey for you—in the Sample Session plans! So you know a little more about how the processes play out for Brownies, here's a quick summary:

Girl Led means girls play an active part in figuring out the *what, where, when, how,* and *why* of their activities. Encourage them to lead the planning, decision-making, learning, and fun as much as possible. This ensures that girls experience leadership opportunities as they prepare to become active participants in their communities. With Brownies, you could:

- Help girls make informed choices by talking them through decisions

- Encourage girls to add their own flair to projects and activities

- Give girls the freedom to solve problems on their own

Learning by Doing engages girls in continuous cycles of action and reflection that result in deeper understanding of concepts and mastery of skills. As they participate in activities and then reflect on them, girls explore their own questions, gain new skills, and share ideas. It's important for girls to connect their experiences to their lives and apply what they have learned to future experiences in and outside of Girl Scouting. With Brownies, you could:

- Encourage them to answer their own questions through hands-on activities

- Ask girls to do more than they are capable of doing on their own while offering limited, but strategic, help

- Offer opportunities for girls to engage their motor skills and their senses

Cooperative Learning has girls work together toward goals with mutual respect and collaboration. Working together in all-girl environments encourages girls to feel powerful and emotionally and physically safe, and allows them to experience a sense of belonging. With Brownies, you could:

- Make the most of teamwork activities

- Encourage girls to decide as a team how to accomplish a task

- Demonstrate giving others equal opportunity to participate in decisions

KEEP IT GIRL LED

Yes, Brownies can take the lead! From beginning to end, keep your eye on what the girls want to do and the direction they seem to be taking. It's the approach begun by Juliette Gordon Low: When she and her associates couldn't decide on a new direction, she often said, "Let's ask the girls!"

Girl-led experiences are built right into this journey to make it easy for you. At each session, ask the girls for their own thoughts on what they've done or discussed.

DON'T RUSH!

Give the girls (and yourself!) some quiet time throughout the journey to stop, think, talk, and reflect. Resist the urge to rush from "doing" to "more doing," and try to follow the discussion tips and questions provided to assist the Brownies in getting deeper meaning from what they have just done.

What It All Means for Girls

All activities in this leadership journey relate to Discovering, Connecting, and Taking Action—the three Girl Scout keys to leadership! Plus, Girl Led, Learning by Doing, and Cooperative Learning processes make the activities fun and powerful for girls. Here, in an activity from Session 2, you can see how these processes and the national Girl Scout outcomes—the benefits we want for girls—play out during a team gathering. Throughout *A World of Girls*, you'll see processes and outcomes play out again and again. Before you know it, you'll be using these valuable aspects of Girl Scouting in whatever Brownies do!

FROM SAMPLE SESSION 2

Me and My Girl Worlds

In this activity, the girls go deeper in understanding their own worlds and the women and girls who are part of those worlds. To begin, give each girl a sheet of paper and markers. Get the Brownies started with these directions:

- Draw a circle that takes up most of the paper, fold the paper into quarters, and then unfold the paper. The circle stands for your world.

- In each quarter of the circle, write or draw one of the groups of girls or women who are part of your world. (Possible groups: Brownies; girls and women in a girl's family; girls and women at school; girls on the bus; girls in an after-school activity such as a team or dance class.)

Right from the start, girls are leading the way—by naming their "girl worlds." This is an example of the **Girl Led** process for this age. Having girls fold the paper and write names of or draw groups of girls or women who are part of their world is also a great way to get girls **Learning** (to identify those in their world) **by Doing**.

As girls share what they like about being part of a girls' or women's group, they are positively identifying with their gender and progressing toward the **Discover outcome, Girls develop a strong sense of self**.

After the girls have drawn their groups, invite each to choose one of them and explain what she likes about it and how she feels when she is with this group. You can tie this activity to the "Picturing Your World of Girls," "Women in My World" and "Tell Your Stories Again and Again" activities in the *GIRLS* side of the Brownies' book.

Each of these activities also moves girls toward the **Connect outcome, Girls feel connected to their communities, locally and globally**, as they begin to recognize the importance of being part of a larger community of girls and women.

team talk!

Ask: *What stories have you learned from the women and girls in your family? What favorite things have you learned about? Were you surprised by the many groups of girls in your world? In what ways are you a leader in any of the groups* (on the bus, in the lunchroom, on a team, etc.)?

These questions guide girls in starting to reflect on what they have learned through this activity, and are an example of the latter part of the **Learning by Doing** cycle.

This last question specifically might help girls feel they have important leadership roles and responsibilities—in places they had not considered before, and advances them on the **Take Action outcome, Girls feel empowered to make a difference in the world**.

Girl Scout Traditions and Ceremonies

Traditions and ceremonies have always been part of the fun of being a Girl Scout. They show girls they are part of a sisterhood: They connect girls to one another, to their sister Girl Scouts and Girl Guides around the world, and to the generations of girls who were Girl Scouts before them.

Along this journey, you'll find many opportunities for the Brownies to enjoy rhymes, gather in Friendship Circles, and hold award ceremonies. Ceremonies give the girls a chance to share their strengths, hopes, and accomplishments, and experience the power of belonging. So involve the girls in creating new traditions—even silly songs! Your Girl Scout council may have its own traditions that you can enjoy, too. Here are a few of the most enduring Girl Scout traditions:

GIRL SCOUT SIGN

The Girl Scout sign is made when saying the Girl Scout Promise. The sign is formed with the right hand, using the thumb to hold down the little finger, leaving the middle fingers extended to represent the Promise's three parts.

QUIET SIGN

The Quiet Sign is a way to silence a crowd without shouting at anyone. The sign is made by holding up the right hand with all five fingers extended. It refers to the original Fifth Law of Girl Scouting: A Girl Scout is courteous.

GIRL SCOUT HANDSHAKE

The Girl Scout handshake is the way many Girl Guides and Girl Scouts greet each other. They shake their left hands while making the Girl Scout sign with their right hand. The left-handed handshake represents friendship because the left hand is closer to the heart than the right.

FRIENDSHIP CIRCLE

This circle is often formed at the end of meetings or campfires as a closing ceremony. Everyone gathers in a circle, and each girl crosses her right arm over her left and holds hands with the person on each side. With everyone silent, the leader starts by squeezing the hand of the person next to her. One by one, each girl passes on the squeeze until it travels around the full circle.

GIRL SCOUTS!

As Girls Scouts celebrates its 100th anniversary in 2012, this leadership journey is a reminder of the long-cherished Girl Scout tradition of girls creating change in their local and global communities. *It's Your Story—Tell It!* continues the story of Girl Scouting—a story of leadership and making the world a better place.

GIRL SCOUT DAYS TO CELEBRATE

- **Founder's Day**
  October 31
  Juliette "Daisy" Gordon Low's birthday

- **World Thinking Day**
  February 22
  A day for Girl Scouts and Girl Guides throughout the world to think about one another

- **Girl Scout Birthday**
  March 12
  The day in 1912 when Juliette Gordon Low officially registered the organization's first 18 girl members in Savannah, Georgia

Your Perspective on Leadership

The Girl Scout Leadership keys—Discover + Connect + Take Action—demonstrates that leadership happens from the inside out. Your thoughts, enthusiasm, and approach will influence the Brownies, so take a few minutes now—and throughout the journey—to apply the three "keys" of leadership to yourself.

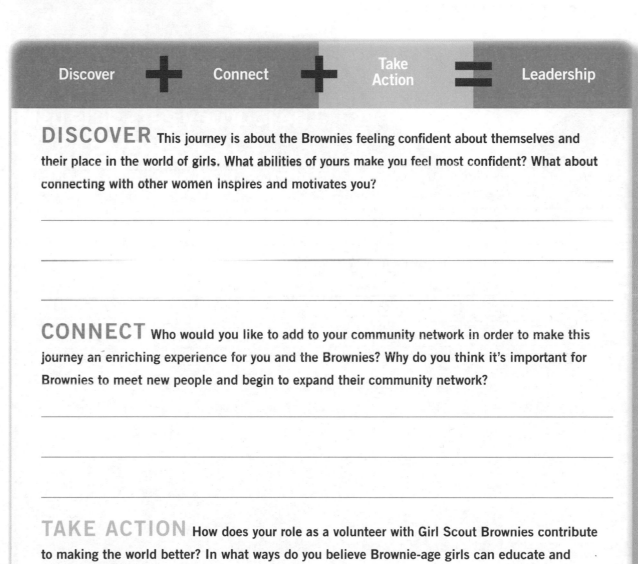

Discover	**+**	Connect	**+**	Take Action	**=**	Leadership

DISCOVER This journey is about the Brownies feeling confident about themselves and their place in the world of girls. What abilities of yours make you feel most confident? What about connecting with other women inspires and motivates you?

_____

_____

CONNECT Who would you like to add to your community network in order to make this journey an enriching experience for you and the Brownies? Why do you think it's important for Brownies to meet new people and begin to expand their community network?

_____

_____

TAKE ACTION How does your role as a volunteer with Girl Scout Brownies contribute to making the world better? In what ways do you believe Brownie-age girls can educate and inspire others to make the world a better place?

_____

_____

Every session in this journey has been created to help girls become **confident leaders—** in their own lives and in the world!

How?

The journey gets girls using the **3 keys** to leadership: **Discover, Connect, and Take Action.**

Girls **Discover** themselves.

They **Connect** with others.

And they **Take Action** in the world!

And in every session of the journey, **girls lead, team up, and learn by doing.** (And you'll learn right along with them. Have a wonderful journey!)

For more on the leadership keys and Girl Scout processes and their benefits to girls, see pages 20–21 and 102–104 in this guide, and *Transforming Leadership: Focusing on Outcomes of the New Girl Scout Leadership Experience* (GSUSA, 2008) and *Transforming Leadership Continued* (GSUSA, 2009). Both publications are available on girlscouts.org.

JOURNEY SNAPSHOT

SESSION 1 Girls Around the World	The Brownies are introduced to the journey and its awards. They start a Team Passport, play games from around the world, and explore how games and stories link them to a wider world of girls.
SESSION 2 Girls in Our World	The Brownies see how they belong to many circles, or "worlds," of girls, and explore how stories of women and girls often hold clues about actions they can take to make the world better. They earn their Hear a Story Award.
SESSION 3 From Story Clues to Story Change	The Brownies explore how they can use clues to create change in their world, play relay games to create stories, and experience and appreciate diversity in the world.
SESSION 4 Planning for Change a Story	The Brownies begin to make a positive change in the world around them as they start their Change a Story project. They use role-play scenarios to practice communication skills, make and enjoy healthful *bento* snacks, and get active with a team dance.
SESSIONS 5 & 6 Change a Story: Making It Happen	Brownies team up to carry out their project. They create self-portraits to express their uniqueness, act out favorite stories in story charades, and explore clues for change in a story about Juliette Gordon Low.
SESSIONS 7 & 8 Planning and Telling Our Story of Change	The Brownies earn their Change a Story Award and then plan for and present their story of change, and inspire their audience to keep that change going. They also explore stories in advertising and media, and create their own ads.
SESSION 9 Our Whole Story	The Brownies consider their place in the world of girls and plan their final journey celebration. They earn their Tell a Story Award, and create a team quilt that expresses their own strengths and tells the story of their Brownie world of girls.
SESSION 10 World of Girls Celebration	The Brownies celebrate their place in the world of girls with their own artistic creations and think about all they've done along the journey. They also say what they want for themselves and the world of girls going forward. They earn their Better World for Girls! Award.

SAMPLE SESSION 1
Girls Around the World

AT A GLANCE

Activities in this session launch the journey's two intertwining themes: the world of girls and the power of stories.

You might set up the session as a special journey kickoff and invite your Friends and Family Network and any Cadettes interested in earning their LiA Award by working with Brownies. That way, everyone starts the journey together!

Crunched for time? Save "Our Globe (or Map) of Girls" for the second gathering. Or simply spread the fun across two sessions—however it suits the girls! You'll know best what will get the Brownies excited about *A World of Girls*!

Goal: The Brownies have fun exploring how stories and games can link them to the wide world of girls—and how they belong to this wide world of girls, too!

- **Opening Ceremony: A Circle of Adventure**

- **Introducing the Journey's Awards**

- **Team Passport**

- **Games Around the Globe**

- **"Flying into Shali's Desert Home"**

- **Snack Time: Jordan's Refreshments**

- **Closing Ceremony: A Great Place!**

MATERIALS

- **Team Passport:** paper, markers, and assorted art materials

- **Games Around the Globe:** for *Banyoka*, large objects for obstacles (desks, chairs, books or boxes, traffic cones, large balls); for *Cencio Mollo*, a handkerchief

- **Our Globe (or Map) of Girls:** globe or world map, sticky notes or slips of paper, tape, yarn, or thread; computer with Internet access (optional, to show the WAGGGS Web site, see page 33)

- **Snack Time:** pita bread, hummus, cut vegetables for dipping; figs or Fig Newtons

PREPARE AHEAD

Talk with any Network members, and Cadettes or other assistants, about their roles for this opening gathering.

Opening Ceremony: A Circle of Adventure

Gather the girls in a circle and welcome them to this journey called *A World of Girls*. You might say something like:

- *Today we're beginning an exciting journey called* A World of Girls. *You may already know what a journey is. Can anyone tell us? That's right, it's an adventure where you meet new people, see new places, learn new things, and have fun!*

- *On this journey, we'll learn about the lives of girls all over the world. You'll also explore your own world and the girls in it—your families, your friends, and girls from all parts of your life.*

- *How will we do all this? Through stories! We'll hear, read, and talk about stories of women and girls. You'll see that stories have clues in them about how to make the world a better place.*

Then say something like: *Now, let's link arms and imagine that we're forming a circle around the world, and let's say the Girl Scout Promise and the Girl Scout Law together.*

Then start a brief discussion with points like these:

- *We've just said the Girl Scout Promise and the Girl Scout Law, two wonderful things that unite Girl Scouts all around the world.* (See inside front cover for the full text of the Promise and Law.) *Did you notice how the last line of the Law asks you to "be a sister to every Girl Scout"?*

- *What do you think it means to be "a sister" to all the girls in our Brownie group, and all the Brownies around the world?* (If the girls don't answer right away, offer suggestions such as: caring about and learning about one another, having fun together, sharing ideas and feelings.)

Introducing the Journey's Awards

Let the girls know that on this journey, they'll earn four awards: Hear a Story, Change a Story, Tell a Story, and Better World for Girls! You might point out the pictures of the awards on page 7 of the *GIRLS* side of their book and say: *We'll talk more about these awards as we travel along. For now, let's get started on this fantastic journey!*

IT'S A BIG CIRCLE!

When you add up 720,000 Brownies, plus all the other Girl Scouts, and then all the Girl Guides around the world, the number is in the millions—and counting. That's a wonderfully wide world of girls!

MORE ON AWARDS!

The journey's awards are detailed on page 12 of this guide and on page 7 of the GIRLS side of the Brownies' book. You'll have a chance to talk more about them with the Brownies in later sessions.

The steps to earning the awards—and suggested award ceremonies—are built into the journey's Sample Sessions.

Page 7, *GIRLS* side of the Brownies' book

Team Passport

The girls' book includes Passport pages that give the Brownies a place to track all they do to earn their awards (see pages 38–40 in the *GIRLS* side of the book). Point the girls to those pages and invite them to create a Team Passport, too, to capture the story of what they do together all along the journey. For girls who don't know what a passport is, you might explain it this way:

- *A passport is a little booklet, much like a big ticket, that lets you go places around the world. And each time you go to a new place, you get your passport stamped with the name of the place you visited. So, with those stamps in it, a passport tells the story of your travels.*

- *Our Team Passport is going to tell the story of this Girl Scout journey we're taking together!*

Get the girls started on planning what type of Team Passport they want to make by sharing the ideas below or others you and the girls might have. If materials are handy, the Brownies can get started right now! Keep the Passport in your care between sessions, or have the girls take turns being the "Passport Keeper."

GO ALL OUT FOR THE TEAM PASSPORT

The Team Passport is meant to be a highly imaginative take on a passport, so there's no one, right way to create it. In fact, it needn't look like a standard passport at all. Let the girls' imaginations run wild!

What the Brownies add to the passport at each gathering needn't be consistent. Artistic quality is not important either. Team fun is the priority!

Decorate a box like a travel case. Have the girls cover a box with maps or postcards, and then fill it with items they've made or chosen that reflect their experiences all along the journey.

Make a photo album or photo display. At each gathering, have one or two girls take photos of the group. Start a sign-up sheet for individuals or pairs to take turns being the photographer. Reach out to your Friends and Family Network (see page 16) for a camera the girls can share and an inexpensive way to print photos. As each new gathering begins, the girls can post photos from the previous session and write captions for them.

Use sheets or a roll of paper. Each time the girls meet, they might mark off a panel and fill it in with stickers, rubber stampings, drawings, writing, pictures, photos—whatever they choose. The panels might be titled and numbered, like chapters in a storybook or panels in a comic strip, and taped together as the journey progresses.

Create a diorama. As a team, the girls might design the background of a diorama, and then add toy figures, cutouts, or other items each time they get together.

ACTIVE TIME

Games Around the Globe

Next, talk with the girls about games and how much fun they can be. You might say:

- *All around the world, girls like to play games, especially games in which they move around.*

- *Playing games together is a way to get to know others, and active games are important for staying healthy and fit.*

- *By playing games from around the world, you also get to see what girls in other places like to do.*

Then ask the girls to name some games they enjoy and to tell what they like about them. After each girl has a chance to share her favorites, invite the group to play *Banyoka* or *Cencio Mollo* (described below), or another game that you know from a country other than your own.

Banyoka, an obstacle-course game, can be played indoors or out. Indoor obstacles can include furniture, stacks of books or boxes; outdoor ones can be traffic cones, large balls, or boxes. To play the game:

- Form two teams of equal numbers of girls.

- Each team becomes a "snake": The girls sit on the floor or ground, one behind the other, with their legs open like scissors and their hands on the shoulders, or their arms around the waist, of the girl in front.

- Each team "scootches" along, moving around or over the obstacles while staying connected. The first team to get around its set of obstacles wins.

Variations: The girls form their snake by standing, with arms linked sideways. Or they play as one team, navigating against the clock through a set of obstacles.

Cencio Mollo: In this traditional Italian game, the girls form a circle and one girl is chosen to be "It."

- The girl who is "It" stands in the center with a handkerchief and goes to someone in the circle and says, "The *Cencio Mollo* has come to you."

- The girl she is facing says, "Let it come. I shall not cry, laugh, or kiss it." Then the "It" girl tries to make her laugh any way she can, but she can only touch her with the handkerchief on the head or face.

- If the player doesn't laugh, "It" moves on to the next girl in the circle. If the player laughs, she pays a penalty, such as having to sing a song, jump in the air five times, or do something else silly. Then she becomes "It."

GAMES & STORIES!

Games are like stories! They play out over time with a beginning, a middle, and an end. You might get the girls talking about a game after they play it: First we did this, then this happened and that happened, and then our team won. That's a story!

WHAT'S IN A GAME'S NAME?

Banyoka comes from the African countries of Zambia and Zaire, and means "the snake."

Cencio Mollo (pronounced *CHEN-cho-MOL-lo*) is Italian for wet handkerchief.

WANT MORE GLOBAL GAMES?

Other international games can be found on the Internet or in books.

Escargot, for example, is a French version of hopscotch in which the jumping path is a spiral shape, like a snail.

Kongki Noli is a variation of jacks played in Korea. Instead of a ball and jacks, small stones are used.

"Sky tossing" is a traditional Inuit game. One person stands in the middle of a large animal skin, while others stand in a circle, grab the edge of the skin, and pull hard on it. The skin snaps up, sending the person into the air, as if she were on a trampoline. The game is also played with blankets.

ENCOURAGE MANY CONNECTIONS!

If the girls want to identify more than one country connection, encourage them to do so! They may . . .

● have visited the country

● have relatives there

● have friends from there

● like the food or music of a particular country

● know a story set there

After the girls play a game, ask them how they liked it. You might also ask: *How are these games like games you already play? How are they different?*

Then explain that some games have a little story inside them. For example, in *Cencio Mollo* or other games of tag, when you're "It," you're in a situation you try to get out of. And the story of *Banyoka* is about finding your way around any obstacles that might block your path.

Ask the girls to describe the stories inside some games they play, including any games they've made up on their own. Share with the girls that games found around the world are like the variations that happen with stories: Games get passed along, culture to culture—just like the many versions of a story, like "Cinderella," for example, that can be found all around the world.

Our Globe (or Map) of Girls

Show the girls a globe (or map) of the world and introduce them to the idea that they're connected to other girls in other countries all around the world. If the girls played the handkerchief game, point out Italy—that's one connection they now have. Then give a few connections of your own, such as:

● *I'm connected to the country of _____, because my grandparents came from there.*

● *I'm connected to _____, because I visited there in college.*

● *I'm connected to _____, because I love _____ food.*

Then say: *Now it's your turn. Think of a way you are connected to another country, write the connection on a sticky note (or slip of paper), and place it on that country.*

After the girls have put their notes on the globe or map, invite them to take a piece of yarn or embroidery thread and connect that country to their community. Explain that throughout the journey, the girls will add to their world connections.

GIRL SCOUTS AROUND THE WORLD

Continue the mapping activity by asking the girls to point out other countries where they think Brownies might live. Then say: *Girl Scouts or Girl Guides are in more than 145 countries. That means you have a really big sisterhood of girls all around the world!*

If possible, show the girls the Web site of the World Association of Girl Guides and Girl Scouts (wagggs.org), and explain that WAGGGS supports and unites all Girl Guides and Girl Scouts. Supervise them in posting their own comments about being a Brownie. Or simply ask:

- *What is one thing you'd like to learn about Girl Scouts in another country?*

- *And one thing you'd like Girl Scouts in other countries to know about you?*

"Flying into Shali's Desert Home"

Next, get the girls talking about "Flying into Shali's Desert Home," the first story in their book. If the girls have enjoyed other Brownie journeys, they'll know the characters of Campbell, Jamila, and Alejandra. Ask: *What do you remember about these girls?*

Then share some of the information about Jordan, at right, that you think will most interest the girls. Or keep the information handy, in case the Brownies have questions as they hear the story.

Even if the girls have read the story on their own, it's fun to share a story together. So invite the girls to take turns reading all or part of the story aloud. Depending on how far they read, ask some questions like these:

- *What did the Brownie friends learn about Shali's world?*

- *What things do Campbell, Jamila, and Alejandra have in common with Shali?*

- *What do you have in common with her?*

- *What was most interesting to you about Shali's world?*

After the girls share their reactions to Shali and her cousins' lives, invite one to come up to the globe or map to locate Jordan, put a sticky note on it, and say what she most enjoyed learning about girls there. You might guide them first to the Middle East and then help them zero in on the country of Jordan.

JORDAN
Quick Facts

- **Jordan, an Arab country** in the Middle East, is a little smaller than Indiana and borders the countries of Syria, Iraq, Saudi Arabia, and Israel.

- **Western Jordan** is in the valley of the Jordan River, and is the only region where crops can grow. The eastern and southern parts are desert, with fewer than two inches of rain a year.

- **Arabic is the official language,** but most people speak both Arabic and English. People often greet each other by saying *As-Sal¯mu `Alaykum,* which means "peace be upon you." The typical response to that is *Wa `Alaykum as-Salaam,* meaning "and upon you be peace."

- **The biggest city** is the capital of Amman.

- **Jordanians eat** their main meal during the middle of the afternoon.

Snack Time

Jordan's Refreshments

Bring out the hummus and pita bread (along with the cut-up vegetables for dipping), and let the girls know that these are foods eaten in Jordan. If the girls (like the Brownies in the story) have never tasted a fig, have them try one, or a Fig Newton. Get them talking about the cookie's fig "jam" filling and let them know that Fig Newtons were named for the town of Newton, Massachusetts. While they enjoy their snack, they might like to think up treats based on street names, the name of their school, or names of nearby towns.

MORE PASSPORT FUN WITH STORIES!

Before you close, look back with the girls at all the ways they've learned that stories can be told: through games, a "passport," storybooks, maps, and even treats. Do they want to add any more stories, or ways of telling stories, to their Team Passport? Encourage Brownies to have fun continuing to think about stories! Ask them to think about girl characters they know from movies, TV shows, books, cartoons, or other sources. Any thoughts they bring back to their next gathering will help with the journey's many story-related activities.

Closing Ceremony: A Great Place!

To underscore the storytelling theme of this journey, invite the girls to have some fun with the following poem, clapping and reaching out or pointing with their hands to match the words they are saying. They can stand together and each say a line from the poem, repeating all lines until everyone has had a turn. Or they can say the remaining lines in unison, and make up their own gestures.

> *Our journey began today*
> *We reached into worlds faraway*
> *We'll reach even farther*
> *On our adventure to come*
> *As we hear stories about girls*
> *Read stories about girls*
> *And share stories about girls*
> *Like you, and you, and you, and me!*
> *Our world of girls is a great place to be!*

Looking Ahead to Session 2

Next time, the girls will seek out clues for their Hear a Story Award. Revisit the award details on page 12 of this guide, along with "Stories + Their Clues" on page 8. Although clues aren't restricted to storybooks, you might plan to meet at a library—a gold mine for stories and clues! Or reach out to your Network to gather a selection of books, magazines, and other story sources to share at your meeting place. Review the lists on page 9 for suggested stories that hold good clues.

Pages 8–9, *GIRLS* side of the Brownies' book

OPTIONAL FIELD TRIP TO LIBRARY

To prepare, visit the library on your own and ask if the librarian would lead a discussion with the girls about clues in stories and how to find them. The librarian can likely gather various stories from the library's own collection for the girls to discuss and borrow.

- Share with the librarian the "Stories + Their Clues" section of this guide (page 8) and describe the requirements of the Hear a Story Award (page 12). You might also share a copy of the girls' book.

- Invite the librarian to join with the girls at their final celebration, too, so she can learn all that the girls accomplish on the rest of the journey.

OPTIONAL GUEST SPEAKER: A STORY EXPERT

If a library visit isn't an option for your group, invite a librarian, book editor, author, or someone else familiar with children's stories to your meeting, to talk with the Brownies about clues in stories, and to inspire them to find more clues on their own.

IMPORTANT LEADERSHIP LESSONS!

As the Brownies move through this journey, they actively engage in things that all leaders do. They . . .

- are on the lookout for ways they can act to help others

- think about the kinds of problems they can help solve in their community.

In upcoming gatherings, the Brownies and you will go on to choose, plan, Take Action, and also educate and inspire others on good changes in the world.

This illustration, from the *WORLD* side of the Brownies' book, was inspired by the architecture of Amman, Jordan.

SAMPLE SESSION 2
Girls in Our World

MAKING THE MOST OF THE GIRLS' BOOK

The activities and discussions in this session correspond with the first story in the girls' book, "Flying into Shali's Desert Home." Check the start of each Sample Session for more ways to use the girls' book during each gathering!

AT A GLANCE

Goal: The Brownies enjoy seeing how they already belong to so many circles, or "worlds," of girls and women. They go on to explore how stories about women and girls often hold clues about actions they can take to make the world a better place.

- Opening Ceremony: Girls in My World

- Team Passport

- Overlapping Worlds

- Me and My Girl Worlds

- Shali's Story: Finding Clues for Change

- More Story Clues All Around

- Closing Ceremony: Earning the Hear a Story Award

MATERIALS

- **Team Passport:** materials as decided by girls in Session 1

- **Overlapping Worlds:** five or six jump ropes, chalk

- **Me and My Girl Worlds:** sheets of paper, markers, index cards or slips of paper

- **More Story Clues All Around:** photocopies of "Hear a Story, Find a Clue," page 44

- **Closing Ceremony:** Hear a Story awards for each Brownie

PREPARE AHEAD

- Read the "Stories and Their Clues" section of the Brownies' book (*GIRLS* side, page 8) and lay out any stories gathered from your Network, or from your local library (see the Materials list above for "More Story Clues All Around").

- Review with any assistants what they will do before and during the session.

AS GIRLS ARRIVE

Have adult or Cadette assistants team up with the Brownies to talk about story characters they may have thought about since the last time they gathered. Any girls who may not have thought about story characters can get thinking about them now with the larger group.

Opening Ceremony: Girls in My World

Invite the girls into a Friendship Circle and say: *Let's each name one thing you like to do with other girls, whether one friend, members of your family, or a larger group of girls.*

After all the girls have had a turn, ask them to think over what their sister Brownies said and then go around the circle again, with each one saying: *I like to _____, too, just like* [name of another Brownie].

Team Passport

Remind the girls of how they decided to create their Team Passport, which will tell the story of their journey, and get them going on some additions for it, as they planned at their first gathering.

ACTIVE TIME
Overlapping Worlds

To start, have the girls use all but one of the jump ropes on hand to make large overlapping circles on the floor. If enjoying the activity outdoors, they can instead draw overlapping chalk circles on blacktop. Then:

- Invite the girls to stand in the circles, based on the groups they are part of, as you identify each circle, by saying things like: *If you play a sport, stand in this circle. If you sing or play an instrument, stand in this circle. If you take religion classes, stand over here.* (The circles will overlap on the floor or ground because the girls are a part of more than one group.)

- After every girl is in at least one circle, create a final large circle around all of the girls with the one remaining jump rope. Ask: *What does this circle stand for?* Give the girls a few moments to answer, and then say: *Girl Scout Brownies, of course—the group that all of you share!*

Then invite the girls to pick up the jump ropes and take turns jumping. Encourage them to team up to create an easy jump rope song, or use this variation on a traditional chant:

> *All in together, girls
> How do you like the weather, girls?
> If you're in this world, please jump in:
> Sports team, religion class, music class, dance,
> If you can name another one, here's your chance.*

While they're jumping, encourage the girls to call out other "worlds," either specific or general. Possibilities include: Soccer! Band! Gymnastics! Girl Scouts!

Me and My Girl Worlds

In this activity, the girls go deeper in understanding their own worlds and the women and girls who are part of those worlds. To begin, give each girl a sheet of paper and markers. Get the Brownies started with these directions:

- Draw a circle that takes up most of the paper, fold the paper into quarters, and then unfold the paper. The circle stands for your world.

- In each quarter of the circle, write or draw one of the groups of girls or women who are part of your world. (Possible groups: Brownies; girls and women in a girl's family; girls and women at school; girls on the bus; girls in an after-school activity such as a soccer team or dance class.)

After the girls have drawn their groups, invite each to choose one of them and explain what she likes about it and how she feels when she is with this group. You can tie this activity to the Please Tell Me Your Story, So Many Girls, So Many Stories, and Stories of Favorite Things from the girls' book.

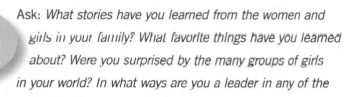

Ask: *What stories have you learned from the women and girls in your family? What favorite things have you learned about? Were you surprised by the many groups of girls in your world? In what ways are you a leader in any of the groups* (on the bus, in the lunchroom, on a team, etc.)?

GIRL WORLDS IN STORIES

Let the girls know that there are girl worlds in stories, too, of course! Pass out the index cards (or slips of paper) and ask them to write the name of a favorite character on one side and one word describing that character on the other side. Some possible examples are: Junie B. Jones: stubborn; Hermione Granger: smart; Jamaica (from the series by Juanita Havill): thoughtful. Ask the girls to bring their card or paper to their next Brownie time together.

If needed, give the girls some time to look through the books and stories on hand. When everyone is ready, give the following instructions:

- *Put your card on the floor near you, with the name of the character face-down.*

GIRLS STUCK FOR WORLDS?

Jot some words on a newsprint or a whiteboard or chalkboard to get the Brownies thinking about all the "worlds" they belong to:

- the school bus
- the school cafeteria
- class
- dance class
- soccer team
- swim club
- Sunday school

and of course, Girl Scouts!

- Walk around the room, read all the words that you see facing up, and stand next to the word that you think best describes you. More than one of you can stand near the same word.

- Now flip over the cards. What character is there? You have something in common with that girl! Do you know or like that character? Are you surprised to think of yourself like [character's name]?

Encourage the girls to compare themselves to more characters, with questions such as:

- What other characters do you think you are like? In what ways?

- Are there any characters in stories you don't want to be like? Why?

If some Brownies aren't familiar with a character, ask the girl who brought in that card to describe the character and her story and tell why she chose it.

Shali's Story: Finding Clues for Change

Now ask the girls: Remember the story about Shali in your book? If you were filling out a card (or paper) to describe Shali, what word or words would you write? (The girls might say friendly or curious.)

Then explain to the girls that today they're going to look for clues in stories. Ask: What's a clue?

The Brownies might say a clue helps you find something or solve a mystery. Respond by saying something like:

That's right! It's exciting to find things and solve mysteries.

Then say: Today we're going to look for a clue in Shali's story.

> **TAKE TIME TO ENJOY THE STORY!**
>
> The girls have likely read the story on their own, but they might like to share it again together now. So invite them to take turns reading all or part of the story aloud.

Get the girls started by asking some questions and making some points like these:

- *What is something in Shali's life that she wants help with?* (Answer: She wants to be a better reader. She said that some books are just too hard for her.)

- *So that's a clue! It's something we can find in a story that could be changed for the better!*

- *Is this something we could help Shali with? How?*

Also remind the girls that Grandmother Elf says she has a way to help Shali: She thinks she can find books that are "just right" for her.

Next, get the girls thinking about how this clue might apply to their own lives. Say something like:

- *The clue in this story is that two of the girls, Shali and Campbell, want to read better.*

- *Do you think anyone you know also wants to be able to read better? Could we do anything to make things better for them?*

Get the girls thinking about what they might do. Ask them for ideas for how to get children to become better readers. Suggest to them:

- setting up a reading-buddies program for students who struggle with reading

- finding ways to get really fun-looking books to children so they will want to read more and get better at it

- reading to younger children, so they can learn more (and become great readers themselves!)

After the girls come up with some more ideas, say something like:

These are all great ideas. And following through on ideas like these is a way to make the world better for girls. That's how a clue in any story can lead to a good change you can make in your own world!

GOING DEEPER INTO "GIRL WORLDS"

In this activity, the girls go deeper in understanding their own worlds and the women and girls who are part of them. You can tie what the girls do to these activities in the *GIRLS* side of their book:

- Clues Close to Home, page 12

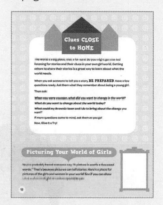

- Women in My World, page 13

- So Many Worlds of Girls, page 17

- All Our Stuff Has Stories, page 20

- Girls in the World, page 35

More Story Clues All Around

Offer a few more examples of clues to be found in stories, using the stories listed below, or other stories you know. Or check the "How Brownies Find Clues!" section on page 9 of this guide.

- Mallory, in *Back to School, Mallory*, by Laurie B. Friedman, has to adjust when she moves to a new school. Being new sometimes feels awkward and lonely—that's a clue.

- Laura from *Little House on the Prairie*, by Laura Ingalls Wilder, is snubbed by some girls in town because her clothes aren't as nice as theirs. That's a clue!

- Little Red Riding Hood was not safe when she walked alone to her grandmother's house. That's a clue, too!

- Satsuki, the Japanese girl in the movie "My Neighbor Totoro," written and directed by Hayao Miyazaki, is worried about her mother being in the hospital. So that's another clue!

Then let the girls know that stories with clues are everywhere: in TV commercials and TV shows, in the stories that were shared with the girls by the women in their families (Brownies' book, *GIRLS* side, page 13), in comic strips, on cereal boxes, or on the packaging of toys and games. Encourage the girls to look and listen for clues in all kinds of stories.

Now, let the Brownies know that to earn their Hear a Story Award, they will each try to find a clue in a story. Pass out copies of the "Hear a Story, Find a Clue" work sheet (page 44) and ask the girls to fill it out by choosing a story they like and finding a clue for change in that story. Encourage the girls to assist each other in finding clues if they get stuck!

The girls might recall a TV show or movie and a clue from it. They might listen for clues (if stories are read aloud) or find them among the books, magazines, and materials you've gathered. If a story is too long for the girls to read completely at this session, give them a quick summary of it, if possible.

When the girls have filled out their sheets, collect them and congratulate the girls on their amazing clue-finding. Then tell them to "stay tuned." There's more clue fun coming next time they get together!

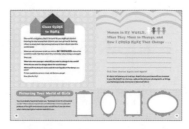

Pages 12–13, *GIRLS* side of the Brownies' book

THESE CLUES WILL COME IN HANDY

Keep in mind that the clues the girls find will come in handy in later sessions of the journey. Right now, you are simply guiding the Brownies to think of all the clues available about how they can make the world better. And that's important, too!

HEAR A STORY, FIND A CLUE

My name: ....

Title of the story I chose: ....

The clue I found in this story: ....

Where I heard or read the story: [check box]

❏ Book   ❏ Magazine ad   ❏ Movie   ❏ TV show

❏ Cartoon   ❏ Comic strip   ❏ Game   ❏ Other

Name of girl character in the story: ....

Names of other girls in the story: ....

A change I'd like to create in the story to make the character's world better:

....

....

....

I am an Amazing
Clue Finder!

....

....
[your name]

Earning the Hear a Story Award

Gather the girls in a Brownie Circle and say: *Today we've learned about clues in stories, and we also learned about our many worlds of girls.*

Congratulate the girls on being great clue finders! Let them know that by finding clues in stories, they've earned their Hear a Story Award— the first leadership award on this journey.

As you present the girls with their awards, invite each one to say a line, in turn, from the following rhyme, until all the girls have spoken.

> *Did you hear a story that had a clue?*
>
> *Did you read one, was it new?*
>
> *I found a story, and so did you!*
>
> *I found a clue, and you did, too!*

Then give the girls a few minutes to fill in their passport/award tracker (page 38 in their book), while you sign, stamp, or sticker each one, with great ceremony!

EARNING THE FIRST AWARD

Clue-finding and digging into stories is fascinating, so the girls may want to find more than one clue. Cheer them on! And let them know that what they are doing to earn this award is something all great leaders do:

- They are finding ways they can act to help others.

- They are thinking about the kinds of problems they can help solve in their community.

So they are leaders, too!

Looking Ahead to Session 3

Call on your Network to gather peppers of various shapes, sizes, colors, and heat for the next session. Suggest that they also provide a healthful dip (such as a dip of pureed chickpeas, sweet red peppers, plain yogurt, and herbs to taste).

Keep the "4 Brownie Awards" chart handy!

Now that girls have earned the Hear a Story Award, you'll be starting to guide them to their Change a Story and Tell a Story awards. All the steps to these awards are built right into upcoming sessions of the journey.

As you and the girls journey forward, you'll likely find it helpful to keep in mind the big picture of how the journey invites girls to go from "hearing" many clues (each Brownie has found her own) to making a team decision about one clue they will act on together. By creating a plan and acting on this one clue together, they will actually be "changing a story" and helping others. Then they will "tell the story" of that change in order to inspire others to make the world better, too.

So, on this journey, the "tell the story" helps Brownies learn one way to create change that goes beyond a one-shot event. By giving others a call to action, they can keep their "Change a Story" effort going! And each of the four awards for girls represents one part of the whole big journey!

The chart on the opposite page helps you see how everything fits together and gives you some examples of what girls might do to earn their awards, too. Remember, though, they are just examples. You and the girls will shape your very own project! So use the chart throughout the journey as you guide the girls through the steps to their awards.

4 BROWNIE AWARDS THAT ALL FLOW TOGETHER!

examples of how the girls might step through them all

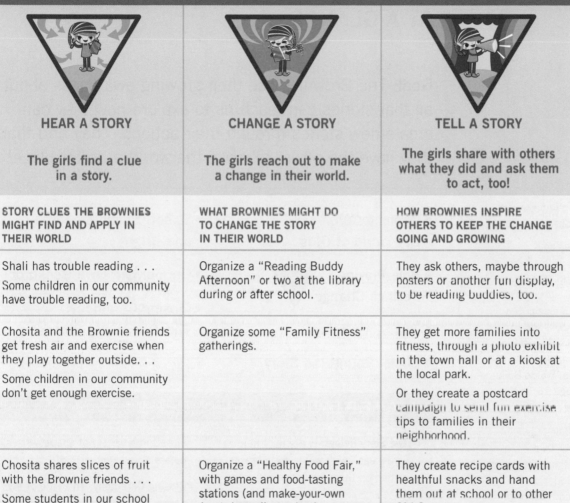

HEAR A STORY	CHANGE A STORY	TELL A STORY
The girls find a clue in a story.	The girls reach out to make a change in their world.	The girls share with others what they did and ask them to act, too!
STORY CLUES THE BROWNIES MIGHT FIND AND APPLY IN THEIR WORLD	WHAT BROWNIES MIGHT DO TO CHANGE THE STORY IN THEIR WORLD	HOW BROWNIES INSPIRE OTHERS TO KEEP THE CHANGE GOING AND GROWING
Shali has trouble reading . . . Some children in our community have trouble reading, too.	Organize a "Reading Buddy Afternoon" or two at the library during or after school.	They ask others, maybe through posters or another fun display, to be reading buddies, too.
Chosita and the Brownie friends get fresh air and exercise when they play together outside. . . Some children in our community don't get enough exercise.	Organize some "Family Fitness" gatherings.	They get more families into fitness, through a photo exhibit in the town hall or at a kiosk at the local park. Or they create a postcard campaign to send fun exercise tips to families in their neighborhood.
Chosita shares slices of fruit with the Brownie friends . . . Some students in our school don't eat healthy snacks.	Organize a "Healthy Food Fair," with games and food-tasting stations (and make-your-own *bento* boxes!) at school.	They create recipe cards with healthful snacks and hand them out at school or to other Girl Scouts.

After Hear a Story, Change a Story, and Tell a Story, the Brownies understand their place in the world of girls! They're ready to earn the BETTER WORLD FOR GIRLS! Award — by telling their story, their way, at their final celebration.

SAMPLE SESSION 3

From Story Clues to Story Change

AT A GLANCE

Goal: The Brownies use their growing awareness about all that stories can teach us to explore how they can create new stories through their actions. They find that they have the power to make the world a better place!

MAKING THE MOST OF THE GIRLS' BOOK

The activities and discussions in this session correspond to "Girls Teaching Girls," page 17, in the *GIRLS* side of the Brownies' book, and to "All Our Stuff Has Stories!" page 20 and "Words Start Stories, Words Build Stories!" page 26, in the *GIRLS'* side.

If girls are doing the optional "Our Own Bookmobile" activity, point them to "Stories on the Go," (*WORLD* side, page 16), and to the *GIRLS* side for "Inventions Are Stories That Change Things for the Better!" page 21, and "The Story of the Real Paper Bag Princess!" page 22.

Pages 16–17, *GIRLS* side of the Brownies' book

- Opening Ceremony: Our World of Girls

- Role-Playing Positive Change

- Two Story Relays

- Circle 'Round the Story

- Sweet, Spicy, Smooth, and Bright

- Option: Our Own Bookmobile

- Closing Ceremony: The Title of My Story

MATERIALS

- **Two Story Relays:** two sets of index cards, each with words and phrases written on them (see page 50)

- **Sweet, Spicy, Smooth, and Bright:** selection of peppers, both hot and sweet, in a variety of shapes, sizes, colors

- **Closing Ceremony: The Title of My Story:** Team Passport and assorted art materials

PREPARE AHEAD

Write the words and phrases for the "Two Story Relays" activity on the cards (see page 50), and mix up the cards.

Opening Ceremony: Our World of Girls

Gather the girls in a Brownie Circle and invite each girl to name one new thing she's learned about the world of girls on this journey so far. If they need a prompt, you might have them peek at their Team Passport. Or drop some hints about how they asked women in their families about their stories (as their book suggests), about girls in Jordan (or other countries), about the library (if they went there), and so on. Wrap up by saying something like: *Our world of girls gets more and more interesting as we move through this journey!*

Role-Playing Positive Change

Now that the girls know how to spot clues in stories, get them thinking about their ability to create change in their own worlds based on those clues. Invite them, individually or in small groups, to role-play what the girls in stories they know faced and solved or made better. Or if your group would rather draw, suggest that they make a quick sketch of what the girl characters did.

As the entire Brownie team watches girls (or pairs or teams of girls) role-play, invite them to look for the positive changes taking place in the lives of the girls in these stories.

Guide the girls to understand that positive changes like the ones they found in stories and now see in their own role-plays might make the everyday lives of girls better right in their community. Then wrap up by saying something like:

- *We see clues in stories every day that remind us of things in our own community that we can make better.*

- *So be on the lookout, wherever you go, for stories with clues that might show up in your community, too.*

- *Next time we get together, we'll pick one clue that we can all act on together to make our world better.*

ROLE-PLAY STARTERS

If the girls are stuck about which stories to role-play, get them thinking about typical story scenarios in which a character . . . .

- shows kindness to a friend or pet

- shows respect to herself or others

- makes someone feel special

- makes sure she gets some exercise

- thinks before she speaks

Also remind them of specific stories they discussed in previous gatherings, as well as the stories about the Brownie friends and their travels in their book.

Two Story Relays

STORIES ON THE GO!

These two relay races get the girls up and about as they put words together to create stories.

RELAY 1

To start, have two sets of cards, each card holding one of the 14 words/ phrases listed below. Be sure to mix up the cards in each set!

Also have a table at one end of the room and a cleared space for running.

- Ask the girls to form two teams.

- Distribute the sets of cards to each team, one card per girl, and ask them not to show their cards to anyone.

- At "Go!" the first girl in line runs to the table, places her card word-side up, runs back, and tags the next girl.

- With every new card that gets laid down, the next girl can see how the Girl Scout Promise is forming. Each girl gets one minute to try to complete one line of the Law; then she runs back to tag the next girl. If a girl can't see a solution to make a line or is stumped, she must pass and run back to tag the next girl. The team that gets the words in the right order first wins.

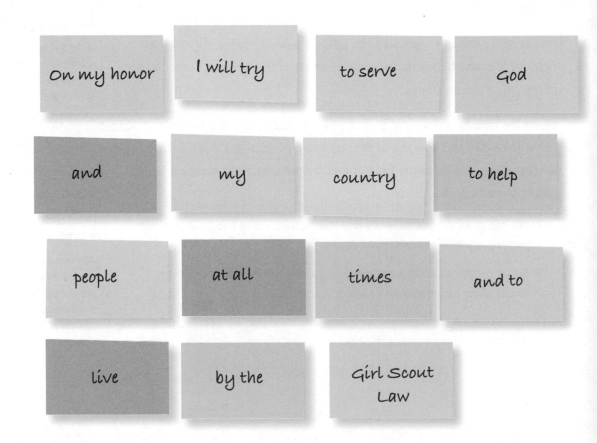

RELAY 2

In this relay, the girls try to create a story from a set of words—any story that makes sense!

Form the girls into new teams and explain these instructions.

- This time, the girls run to the table one at a time and draw two cards from a shuffled deck.

- The first girl places her two words on the table and then runs back, tags the second girl, who runs to the table, chooses two cards and has 15 seconds to place her words with the first two words to start creating a logical story.

- The relay continues with each girl running to the table, choosing two cards from the deck and working to arrange the laid out cards and her cards into a logical story. She can either add to the sentence that is forming on the table, or rearrange it to create something else.

- The relay continues until each girl on each team has had at least two turns at choosing cards and building the story.

- Then, call "time" and ask the girls to read the stories aloud.

- Get the girls talking about what was hard and what was easy about "putting a story together."

Wrap up by reminding the girls that they have more opportunities for oodles of fun with words and stories in their book. Point them to "All Our Stuff Has Stories!" and "Clues Start Stories, Words Build Stories!" on pages 20 and 26, in the *GIRLS* side of their book, for example, and encourage them to enjoy these activities on their own or with friends.

SAMPLE WORDS FOR RELAY 2 CARDS

Once, Upon, a, Time, a, Group, of, Brownies, Found, an, Old, Watch, When, by, Cabin, Went, on, a, Hike, Made, Met, New, Friends, was, in, the, Woods, They, Asked, Where, Saw, Deer, Fox, Waterfall, Built, Fort, Finally, Got, Back, Home, Adventure, the, Trail, Gave, It, to, the, Woman, Her, She, Smiled, They, Wearing, Swam, in, Pond, Felt, Good, at, the, End, of, the, Day, Ran, Jumped, in, Hat, Shoes, Purple, Golden, Cold, the, Beautiful, Mysterious, and

Pages 20–21, *GIRLS* side of the Brownies' book

MAKING UP STORIES ON THE GO!

This activity gives the girls a chance to learn more about stories as they create their own. They might build a story around one of the scenarios below or anything else they dream up!

- A family moves to a new neighborhood with some really amazing neighbors.

- A girl travels to a new place and makes some new friends.

- A girl loses something important and finds it with the help of others.

- A pair or group of friends finds something unusual in a hidden location.

Have the girls come up with a serious story first, and then a funny one, or vice versa.

Circle 'Round the Story

Gather the Brownies in a circle and ask:

- *What makes something a story?* (Possible answers include "interesting characters" and "lots of things happen.")

- Then get the girls talking about how stories are all around them. You might mention the fun of gadgets having stories or favorite objects having stories. (Point them to "All Our Stuff Has Stories!" on page 20, in the *GIRLS* side of their book.)

- Guide the girls to see that stories usually have a beginning, a middle, and an end, and a challenge that the characters have to overcome.

- Invite one girl to make up a sentence that will be the beginning of a story. For example: *One day a girl named Mariah was walking down the street.*

Then, have the girls go around the circle, each adding a sentence to the story.

The sentence from the last girl will be the end of the story.

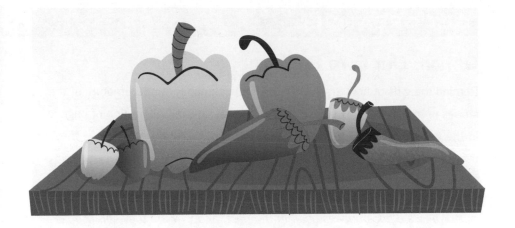

Sweet, Spicy, Smooth, and Bright

In stories and in real life, girls sometimes feel different in some way from others. As a way for the Brownies to experience and appreciate diversity in the world, show them the peppers you've brought of various shapes, sizes, and colors, and degrees of spiciness. Be sure not to lay out the peppers so that similar ones are next to each other (don't put all the red peppers together, for example, or all the short peppers together).

You might say: *Look at these peppers for a bit. They are all related, but each is different, isn't it? Which pepper most reminds you of yourself? Why?*

The girls' answers may reflect their body size and shape differences, their personalities, or other characteristics. (For example: *I'm a redhead, so I choose that pepper.* Or: *I'm small for my age, so I picked that little pepper.* Or: *The green pepper looks bright and shiny, so I chose it because I like to be happy and smile.*)

You might also ask the girls to put the peppers in "families" (based on color, size, shape, personality) and describe how each individual pepper is alike and/or different from the rest of its family. Then ask the girls:

How are you different from or similar to other people in your own family?

Give the girls a chance to taste the peppers, but be sure to warn them about any spicy ones! If your Network helped out with a snack, set it out for the girls while they talk about bookmobiles (see next page).

Page 16, *WORLD* side
of the Brownies' book

Option: Our Own Bookmobile

Remind the girls of how Grandmother Elf's bookmobile is a fun feature of the stories in their book. Point them to the "Stories on the Go" section of page 16 in the *WORLD* side, which explains the history of bookmobiles and how they are used around the world. Ask:

- *Have any of you ever been inside a bookmobile?*

- *Why were bookmobiles used in the past, and why are they still used today?* If the girls don't answer readily, you might give them a hint by saying: *Bookmobiles are a change that makes the world better—what change do you think they bring?* This may prompt the girls to say that bookmobiles get books to people who can't get to a library.

Then, ask the girls to think about an imaginary bookmobile that can travel around the world. Ask:

- *What would the bookmobile look like?*

- *What books would you want to include in it for girls your age all over the world?*

- *Why would you choose those books?*

Guide the girls to generate a group list of the top 10 books for their bookmobile. Encourage them to stand up for any books they think should be included. To focus them further, suggest that they decide on reasons to include the books they choose, such as: "These books show what life is really like for girls," or "These books show girls being strong (or being inventors, leaders, playing sports, or learning about plants and animals . . .)".

TOP TEN BOOKS FOR OUR BOOKMOBILE!

1. _____
2. _____
3. _____
4. _____
5. _____
6. _____
7. _____
8. _____
9. _____
10. _____

BOOKMOBILE MURAL OR MODEL BOOKMOBILE

Remind the girls that they are encouraged, on page 16 in the *WORLD* side of their book, to capture their individual ideas for an amazing bookmobile. You might ask if they'd like to team up to create a mural of their ideal bookmobile and all the places it can travel, and all the books it would hold.

Or ask if the girls might like to create a scale model of their imaginary bookmobile, with the guidance of guest experts in engineering and industrial design. They might also "invent" gadgets for their bookmobile. (Point them to "Inventions Are Stories That Change Things for the Better!" and "The Story of the Real Paper Bag Princess" (about inventor Mattie Knight) in the GIRLS side of their book on pages 21 and 22, respectively. The girls might even want to devote a whole session to making their model. Photograph it, post the image online, or show it to guest librarians and others in your Network—it's one more way to strengthen the Brownies' community connections.

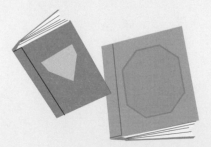

Closing Ceremony: The Title of My Story

Give all the girls a chance to add to the Team Passport. Then gather them in a Brownie Circle and let them have fun with the chant below. They can start it softly and then say it progressively louder:

Every story has a clue!
We find ways to change things, too.

Looking Ahead to Session 4

At the next session, the girls will choose a clue from those they've found to date and plan a positive change for their community. Review the "4 Brownie Awards" chart on page 47. Talk with your Network and other volunteers about what the Brownies might do. Depending on the clues they've found so far, you might talk with teachers, school officials, administrators at places of worship, librarians at public or school libraries, or volunteers who work with Girl Scout Daisies, so that you begin to reach out to possible audiences for the Brownies. Just don't set anything in stone until the Brownies have a chance to do some of their own planning, as built into the next session!

If your Network or your larger community includes someone who knows how to make *bento* boxes, invite her for an in-person demonstration. Plan for the decorated snack foods activity by organizing the preparations in advance and ensuring refrigeration, if needed, at the session. If possible, have a computer with Internet access to share information about *bento* boxes and food designs at: pbs.org/opb/meaningoffood/food_and_family/obento/p2/ or about World Thinking Day: girlscouts.org/who_we_are/global/world_thinking_day/. If having a computer isn't possible, print fun images of *bento* boxes and bring them to show the girls. Or point them to the images on pages 18–19 in the *GIRLS* side of their book.

HOW MUCH TIME? WHICH PROJECT?

Before the girls choose their project, consider how much time you and they have, as well as the extent of your Network support. The girls can achieve a meaningful outcome without a huge effort. What's important is to arrange things so that girls learn about creating lasting change, even if they don't completely do the change themselves.

Look ahead through the tips and project sheets in this session for more support in guiding the girls toward a project that fits their time, resources, and interest.

From Clues to Taking Action

A GOOD PROJECT:

- ☐ is doable
- ☐ meets a genuine need
- ☐ provides a learning experience for the girls that they can share with others

- ☐ uses the "tell a story" opportunity to make a Take Action effort last beyond a one-time change
- ☐ is exciting and fun and something easy enough to share with others
- ☐ inspires others to keep it going

How do clues unfold into successful projects? These tips and the "4 Brownie Awards" chart on page 47 show how!

Think about it! Consider these questions on your own as you guide the girls to narrow their choices and finally choose one clue to Take Action on.

What clues point to a real need for girls in our community?	
Which of the needs appear feasible to act on? What's practical, really?	
Who will benefit from our taking on this project?	

Scale it! The girls can have a powerful and meaningful experience—a story they'll remember and tell over and over—and one that's important to others, with even a modest action.

You might explain this to the girls this way:

We're looking for a project that fits our team "just right." That's one that doesn't involve too many people, or need too many materials or too much equipment. That sounds a little like "The Story of the Three Bears," doesn't it? We'll plan and do the project during our time together. If an idea seems too big to take on, then it's not "just right" for us—and that's OK.

Keep it going! When the girls get to "tell a story," they are putting together their talents and skills to create a change that they and others can keep on going—a change that will last.

The "4 Brownie Awards" chart, on page 47, shows how a one-time change can become a long-lasting change involving others!

Role-playing conflict resolution —that builds social skills and confidence!

SAMPLE SESSION 4

Planning for Change a Story

AT A GLANCE

Goal: The Brownie Team chooses a clue for change that will benefit girls in their community.

MAKING THE MOST OF THE GIRLS' BOOK

Activities and discussions in this session correspond to the second story, "Dancing with Chosita," page 18.

Pages 18–19, WORLD side of the Brownies' book

- Opening Ceremony: Stretching Toward Our Best

- Giving, Sharing, Changing

- Snack Time: Let's Face It . . . No, Let's Eat It! (Option: Thai Lettuce Wraps)

- Saying How It Feels to Me

- Choosing Our Change and Getting Started on It

- Dance It Out

- What If . . . ?

- Closing Ceremony: How Will the Story End?

MATERIALS

- **Giving, Sharing, Changing:** world map and sticky notes

- **Snack Time:** see pages 60–61 for possible ingredients

- **Saying How It Feels to Me:** scenarios on slips of paper (see Prepare Ahead, below)

- **Choosing Our Change and Getting Started on It:** the girls' "Hear a Story, Find a Clue" work sheets from Session 2; photocopies of the "Project Check Sheets" (see pages 66–67)

- **Dance It Out:** Music that the girls can dance to and a music player

- **What If . . . ?:** Team Passport and assorted art materials

PREPARE AHEAD

- Get familiar with the "Dancing with Chosita" story in the girls' book.

- Photocopy the "Saying How It Feels" scenarios on page 62 and cut and fold them, or place them in a bowl or bag. Also copy the check sheets on pages 66–67 for the girls to use as they plan how they will change a story.

- Make a list on chart paper of the clues from the girls' "Hear a Story, Find a Clue" work sheets.

- Gather snack foods for *bento* boxes, or the Thai treats (page 61).

AS GIRLS ARRIVE

- If the girls are passing the Team Passport from one Brownie to the next, invite the girl responsible for it last time to show what she added to it, and make sure the girls know who will add to it after this session.

- Have assistants set up the snack area for "Let's Face It . . . No, Let's Eat It!"

Opening Ceremony: Stretching Toward Our Best

Gather the Brownies in a circle and say something like:

- *Close your eyes, stretch so you are as tall as possible, and think of one thing you are good at.*

- *Then turn to the girl next to you and ask her to name what she thought of, and then switch places in the circle and ask another girl what she thought of.*

- *Keep switching places and asking one another what you're good at, until you've each shared something you're good at with every girl in our group.*

Giving, Sharing, Changing

To get the girls into the mind-set of making a positive change in the world around them, get them talking about "Dancing with Chosita," the story that starts on page 18 in the *WORLD* side of their book.

Ask the girls to open their books to the story, and say something like:

Remember how the three friends joined Chosita in gathering eggs? What other things did they do or talk about that involved giving and sharing? (One possible answer: The Brownie friends recalled a time when they gathered books for libraries and schools damaged by a storm in their country.) These are clues, too!

SHARING SKILLS

This opening ceremony gets the girls sharing their personal talents or skills. It's a great thing for the Brownies to do before they plan their team project because they'll use their skills to shape that project and decide team roles.

THAILAND
Quick Facts

- **Thailand, in Southeast Asia,** is about twice the size of Wyoming. It borders Myanmar, Laos, Cambodia, and Malaysia. Until 1939, Thailand was called *Siam*.

- **Thailand's climate** is mostly hot, humid, and rainy. May to September is monsoon season, when heavy winds bring drenching rains. In 2004, southern Thailand was struck by a tsunami (a giant ocean wave) that damaged coastal areas and killed thousands of people.

- **When Thai people greet one another,** the younger person presses her hands together with her fingertips pointing up, and bows her head so that it touches her hands. This traditional greeting is called a *wai*.

- **Dance is a major art** in Thailand. Classical Thai dance is very complex and has 108 positions for both men and women.

- **Thai food** is known for being spicy. Ingredients in Thai cooking include hot peppers, lime juice, lemongrass, ground peanuts, black pepper, ginger, coconut milk, garlic, sweet basil, and curry. Rice is eaten at almost every meal, and it's often served with fish, pork, chicken, and vegetables.

Continue the idea of giving and sharing as a positive change by asking:

- *What is one way you can give or share at home or at school?*

- *How is your giving or sharing making things better?*

Share something interesting about Thailand, from the Quick Facts at left. Then ask one of the girls to put a sticky note on the world map (or globe), showing where Thailand is located, and say what she most enjoyed learning about girls there.

Snack Time

Let's Face It . . . No, Let's Eat It!

Continue the giving and sharing theme by discussing Makiko (Maki) Itoh, the woman who creates *bento* boxes (see page 19 of the *GIRLS* side of the Brownies' book). If the girls haven't yet read about her, show them the page and say something like:

- Bento *boxes are homemade lunches that many mothers pack for their school-age children in Japan.*

- *Mothers spend a great deal of time making food into fun and appealing shapes, such as little animals, small toys, or funny faces.*

- *Making food that is healthy and fun to look at is one way to show that you care about the people who will eat it.*

Images of *bento* boxes are also on Maki's Web site, justbento.com, or at pbs.org/opb/meaningoffood/food_and_family/obento/p2/.

After the girls see the images of *bento* lunches, invite them to make fun-looking snacks of their own from the assorted healthful foods (such as apple and orange slices, blueberries, pretzels, and crackers) you and your Network have gathered for the session. Other ideas: boiled eggs decorated to look like mice, or a tortilla spread with almond butter (check for allergies!) and then wrapped around a banana and sliced into wheel shapes.

Afterward, invite one girl to place a sticky note on Japan on the globe or world map and say which snack item she enjoyed the most.

OPTION: THAI LETTUCE WRAPS

For this session (or the next), another snack option is a variation of a Thai treat: lettuce wraps. The girls can make them with foods prepared in advance: cooked rice, chopped carrots, celery, and possibly avocado, and hoisin sauce (store-bought, in a jar). The girls can wrap the rice and veggies, along with a little sauce, in a lettuce leaf (such as romaine, butter, or iceberg).

Saying How It Feels to Me

The Brownies are about to team up to plan a project, and they may not always agree on what actions to take. One way they might resolve disagreements is to say how they feel in ways that are true to themselves and yet respectful of others.

Say to the Brownies: *We're going to do a little teamwork for our Change a Story project. There may be times when we don't all agree about what to do. To be a great team, we need to talk and work it out.*

Then, to get the girls thinking about ways to resolve differences, ask some questions like these:

- *When you and a friend want to do different things, what do you do?*

- *How does it feel to tell a friend that you don't want to do what she wants to do?*

- *Can you still be friends with someone even when you don't agree on everything? How so?*

The following role-play situations were created by changing up what actually happens in the stories in the girls' book to create situations where girls have to say something others might not want to hear. Distribute the role-play situations to the Brownies and ask: *What might the girls say in these situations? Let's take turns acting out what they might say and do.*

"SAYING HOW IT FEELS" SCENARIOS

PHOTOCOPY AND CUT ALONG DASHED LINES.

Jamila is tired of jumping rope and wants to do something else in the park.

In the bookmobile, Campbell doesn't want to say that she has trouble reading, too.

Alejandra doesn't want to taste a fig, but she's afraid to say so to Shali's mother.

Campbell becomes sad when she hears about typhoons and hurricanes.

Alejandra would rather read about queens in the bookmobile than play the monkey game, but she doesn't want to seem unfriendly.

Jamila wants to stop fishing and go back to the bookmobile, but she doesn't want to hurt Lakti's feelings.

After the girls have role-played the situations, ask:

- *How did the others react when you finally said something you thought they wouldn't like?*

- *What kinds of feelings did you have while acting out these situations?*

Then add: *Often people don't mind when you disagree with them, if you are respectful of their views and feelings.*

Throughout the journey, encourage the girls to communicate by expressing their true feelings while being respectful of others' feelings.

PROJECT PREPARATION TIPS

Combine the girls' skills and yours with the support of your Network to give the Brownies a powerful learning experience—and a project that has an impact.

Ask around.

Share with your Network what the girls have planned thus far. Reach out into the Girl Scout community. Other adult volunteers may have connections related to the project or its possible location.

Organize the effort.

What will the girls do? What will the Network do? Who among the Network can assist with what? When and where will the project take place? Do you need to chat with school administrators or other officials? (Adapt the "Project Check Sheet: Our Plan," on page 67, as needed.)

Go bigger, go smaller.

The main thing is to keep the excitement and enthusiasm going. If the girls want to do more and have the time—fantastic! If the project has hiccups or too many obstacles, scale it back. Remind the girls that big is not always best.

Roll with it.

The project may not take shape as you and the girls have envisioned it. So be flexible!

Remember the benefits.

This project lets girls strengthen their leadership skills, and their confidence.

COACHING TIPS

- Be sure the girls don't take it personally if their clue is passed over. Praise each clue and avoid making the final choice seem like a winner.

- Take some time for all girls to read or see the story from which the chosen clue was taken. If you don't have time in this session, plan a reading or showing for the start of the next session.

- Let the girls know that whichever project idea they've chosen, they may need to keep other ideas on hand, in case their first choice doesn't pan out.

CHECK IN ALONG THE WAY

As the project moves forward, ensure that girls are learning from what they are doing, meeting new people, building skills, and understanding how they're growing. Set aside time to talk about the progress the team is making. You might ask:

- *What is the best part of what we just did?*

- *What was most useful toward our goal?*

▽ Choosing Our Change and Getting Started on It

Now that the Brownies have thought about ways of giving to others and about speaking up for themselves, it's time to begin their Change a Story project. Explain that together they will choose one clue for change for a project in their community. Bring out the girls' "Hear a Story, Find a Clue" work sheets from Session 2. Ask:

- *Which clues are about something that girls in our community face?*

- *Which clue is something you might like to change in our community? Why?*

- *Is this a change we are excited about creating?*

Guide the girls in narrowing down the number of clues they are considering. Remind them to speak up for the change of their choice—and to listen to other girls express why they prefer an idea. Then, once the girls have a shorter list of ideas, encourage them to review all the clues, so they can come to a decision on one that most of them are happy with.

Once the Brownies have settled on the clue for their project, they'll need some help thinking through the steps to take to create change. Give the girls copies of the Project Check Sheets (pages 66–67). Point out that they've been thinking about stories for much of this journey, and now they'll have a chance to create a new story—the story of a change that they bring to their own community. As you help the girls fill out the first sheet, you might explain how what they are about to do is just like a story. Say something like:

- *The beginning of our story is _____ (the clue we want to change).*
- *The middle of our story is _____ (what we plan to do to make that change).*
- *The end of our story will be _____ (the positive change we will achieve).*

The girls will benefit from your guidance as they fill out their "Project Check Sheet: Our Plan." Don't worry if the Brownies get a little stuck! Teamwork and planning (and changing the world!) are challenging. What matters is that the girls have a great learning-by-doing opportunity and end up with the big points of a plan they feel good about.

You might ask yourself if the Brownies can . . .

- say what they want to do and why it matters to them.
- help think of some of the concrete steps they will need to take.

If so, great! These are skills the girls will use, and build on, all their lives as leaders. You and your Network can fill in some of the nuts and bolts to support the girls. If you find that the girls really like to do their own planning, or just need more time, simply add another meeting to the journey. There's no need to rush the Brownies' learning and accomplishments.

PROJECT CHECK SHEET: OUR STORY

The beginning of our story of change is ....

....

....

....

....

....

The middle of our story is ....

....

....

....

....

....

....

....

We hope the end of our story will be ....

....

....

....

....

....

....

PUTTING IT DOWN ON PAPER

Writing down what they hope the end of their story will be is a great way for the Brownies to think their project through and to say what they want to accomplish.

PROJECT CHECK SHEET: OUR PLAN

☐ What we want to do: ....

☐ How we will do it: ....

☐ Who we will ask to help us: ....

☐ Where we will do it: ....

☐ When we will do it: ....

☐ How we will tell others about it: ....

What each Brownie will do:

NAME	RESPONSIBILITY	NAME	RESPONSIBILITY

What other people will do to assist us:

NAME	RESPONSIBILITY	NAME	RESPONSIBILITY

ACTIVE TIME
Dance It Out

As a break from their planning efforts, remind the girls of Chosita's dance and the carvings of dancing figures in the "Dancing with Chosita" story in the *WORLD* side of their book. Say something like:

- *Dancing is a way that people all over the world express themselves and tell stories.*

- *It's also fun and good for you, because it gets you up and moving.*

Ask the girls to name some things they might do as part of their project. Then invite them to imagine doing one of those things (such as welcoming people to their school, reading to a small child, putting up posters) and act it out as a dance. After several volunteers have had a turn, put on some music and have the girls team up as a group on the dance.

What If . . . ?

Wrap up this session by asking the girls what they think would happen if girls all around the world "changed a story" by doing a project like the one they are planning. Ask questions like:

- *How different could the world be if people everywhere tried to change their communities for the better in some small way?*

- *If lots of people get involved in making a change, would each person's effort have to be very big?*

- *What are some small things people can do that, all together, would make a big difference?*

team talk!

If possible, capture the girls' ideas to share again during award ceremonies and with guests at the journey's final celebration. Suggest that they note their ideas on their Team Passport.

Also, let the girls know that World Thinking Day occurs every year on February 22. Say something like:

This is a day for Girl Scouts and Girl Guides to think about one another and to celebrate friendship—and it's a reminder that you are part of a world of girls!

(For more information, see girlscouts.org/who_we_are/global/world_thinking_day/.)

❀ Closing Ceremony: How Will the Story End?

The project will be more meaningful to the girls if they have a vision of how their community will be changed by their actions. To help make the change more concrete, ask each girl to think about a single (imaginary) girl in the community and to describe what the Brownies' project could mean to that one girl. To get them started, say something like:

I'm imagining a girl named Sandy. She's coming with me to see and hear how we [describe the girls' project here]. This will make one part of her life better—it will [describe change for the better here]. Now, tell me about the girl you have imagined and how her life will be better because of what you will be doing in the community.

Looking Ahead to Sessions 5–6

Sessions 5–6 are combined to give you and the girls the flexibility in time and planning to carry out their Change a Story project. The girls will complete their project plan and go over each girl's responsibilities for it. Ahead of each session, review their plan and confirm everyone's role, and be sure each girl's contribution is included. Check ahead on the time or location of any off-site activities (see the Project Preparation Tips, page 63).

Girls' confidence soars when they realize their small changes can have a big impact.

Change a Story: Making It Happen

EXTENDED PROJECT TIME

Sessions 5 and 6 are set aside as time for the Brownies to focus on their Change a Story project.

Depending on the time the girls have and the nature of what they are doing, they may need one, two, or more sessions to complete their project. They earn their Change a Story Award at the start of Session 7.

The specific activities you and the girls choose for these sessions will depend on their interest and their project. The activities offered here can be enjoyed apart from, and along with, their project. So have fun with what you and the girls have time for—and save the rest for another day!

AT A GLANCE

Goal: The Brownies move ahead with carrying out a team project to benefit girls in their community.

- **Opening Ceremony: Will It Change? We Think It Can!**

- **Carry It Out!**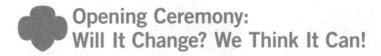

- **Drawing Ourselves (or Option: The Hunt Is On!)**

- **Story Charades and the Power of Stories**

- **Sun and Ice**

- **A Girl Scout Story**

- **Closing Ceremony: My Favorite Part**

MATERIALS

- **Carry It Out!:** the girls' "Project Check Sheets" from Session 4; any materials the girls need to move their plan forward

- **Drawing Ourselves:** large sheets of paper, crayons, colored markers or pencils; or, for **The Hunt Is On!:** photocopies of the scavenger hunt grid, one for each girl (see page 73)

PREPARE AHEAD

Chat with any assistants about what they will do during the session. Photocopy the scavenger hunt grid for "The Hunt Is On!" activity, one copy per girl.

Opening Ceremony: Will It Change? We Think It Can!

Stand in a circle and ask each girl to say one thing that she wants to happen as a result of the change they are making. Then ask the girls to repeat this chant:

We know how the story starts,
For the middle we have a plan.
How it ends is up to us,
Will it change? We think it can!

Carry It Out!

Now's the time for the girls to move their plan forward! They will need time to organize their Change a Story event and any materials or presentations they'll use for it. For example, if they've organized a Reading Buddy Program, they'll need to recruit volunteer readers, schedule time at a library or other public space, and advertise the event by making signs or fliers. They may also assist the volunteer readers by choosing stories to read during the event.

Have the girls work on whatever might be needed for the team's effort. And guide the Brownies to promote good teamwork by:

- encouraging them to take turns
- making sure each girl has a role
- praising girls when you observe cooperation

Be sure to look back over the planning sheets that you completed together at your last gathering. Make sure everyone knows what to expect and what she is doing today (or in a subsequent session). No matter what they're doing, the girls are all acting as leaders as they Change a Story in their own community!

FROM UH-OH TO AHA

If the girls don't feel that their efforts are creating a big enough change, you might explain that important things often start small. Take a look at the sidebar at right and say something like:

- *The clues for change that you found are like seeds. They can grow into mighty trees. So you might not see your results right way, but you can feel good knowing that you have started a change that will last.*

Be sure to point out the passage about seeds and mighty oaks on page 28 in the *GIRLS* side of their book.

AN EXAMPLE OF HOW A CHANGE A STORY EVENT CAN TAKE SHAPE

If the Brownies have planned "Family Fitness" gatherings, they might:

- Tap volunteer yoga or dance teachers, or other fitness experts who can lead demonstrations, or cyclists who can give safety tips

- Arrange time at a local park or gym

- Spread the word about the event by sending invitations or fliers notifying neighborhood or block associations

GIVE THE GIRLS ENCOURAGEMENT AND PERSPECTIVE

Sometimes the nitty-gritty of the Brownies' Change a Story effort may feel small or unimportant. So as they move their Change effort forward, you might remind them that making the world better is often about getting a small snowball moving. They might not see results right away, but they are getting something good started!

What if something the girls had planned to ask for gets a "no" in response? Let the girls know that doesn't mean failure. In fact, success for Brownies comes in the planning for and then making the effort to ask or "make the pitch"—that's what's important. Explain that it's a sign of leadership for the Brownies to be willing to make changes, think again, and keep trying. That's the way to succeed! Then get the girls going on a new plan that will easily change their "uh-oh" into "aha"!

Drawing Ourselves

Start this creative activity by saying something like:

- *We're each going to make a picture of ourselves today.*

- *Your picture won't show what you look like, but it will use colors and shapes to tell a lot about you.*

Get the girls started by giving the following directions, or encourage them to brainstorm their own symbols and meanings, adding labels to their portraits to show what each symbol means.

- *Color your eyes orange if you have no sisters or brothers, purple if you have one or two sisters or brothers, and green if you have three or more.*

- *Make your nose a triangle if you have a pet, and a circle if you don't.*

- *Show three teeth in your mouth if you are 7 years old, four teeth if you are 8, and five teeth if you are 9.*

- *Make your hair straight if you play a sport, curly if you play an instrument or sing, and zigzagged if you like arts and crafts. If all three fit you, your hair can be a mix of all types.*

- *Now add your own necklace that stands for something special about you.*

OPTION: THE HUNT IS ON!

If your group likes being active more than concentrating on art projects, create a scavenger hunt in which each girl gets a grid (see sample on facing page). The girls then go around the room, asking one another questions and filling in the boxes with the names of girls who fall into each category, until each box has at least one name in it. This activity helps the girls recognize how some things are unique to one person (only one person has visited Thailand), but other things may be more common (several girls have pets).

GIRLS AND THEIR WORLD OF GIRLS!

The making of a special self-portrait gives the girls an opportunity to explore what makes each one of them unique and what they have in common. It's a chance for them to explore the Discover key to leadership!

plays soccer	has a cat	tells jokes
was a Daisy	loves jumping rope	can say hello in more than one language
has a baby brother	has a dog	likes maple syrup
has been to another state	has curly hair	has straight hair

LARGE GROUP?

If your group is large and you have assistants, the Brownies might split into two groups for "Story Charades and the Power of Stories."

ADD STORIES TO THE PASSPORT!

The girls might want to list all the stories they act out on their Team Passport. You might say:

Imagine you're in a book club, hearing about stories and talking about stories. Let's keep a list of all the stories you like!

ACTIVE TIME
Story Charades and the Power of Stories

Remind the Brownies that this journey is about stories of girls all around the world. Then ask them to name some of their favorite stories, whether fairy tales or folktales, real-life stories, or stories from books or stories from movies. Examples include *Amazing Grace* and *Princess Grace*, the "Cam Jansen," "Clementine," "Ramona," "Little House," "Golden Compass" or the "Harry Potter" series. (The list of stories on page 9 of this guide might jog their memories.) The girls might also name stories they've read or learned about in school.

Ask the girls to act out part of a favorite story, individually or in pairs or groups, while the other girls guess what the story is. Play these story charades until all the girls have had a chance to act.

Then get the girls talking about the stories they just acted out. Ask some questions like these:

team talk!

- *What did the girl(s) in this story do?* (Aim to get the Brownies seeing the bigger picture: that many characters faced a problem and solved it!)

- *Where did the story take you?* (When actual places are not known, descriptions are fine. To add some movement to this answer, a Brownie can jump to the center of the circle and say the setting of her story, while the other girls spread their arms and "fly" around her.)

- *What was the most exciting part of the story?* (Ask one girl to call out a story name and another to stand and describe what she thinks was most exciting about that story. Invite the girls to clap slowly and softly as she answers. They can speed their clapping as she finishes.)

- *What is the girl in the story like? What do the things she does in the story tell you about her?*

- *Are there things in the story that you would like to change?* (Several girls might answer this question for each story named.)

End by sharing the idea that stories are powerful. Say:

- *We use our imaginations when we read stories.*

- *Stories show us what girls can do.*

- *They give us clues about what we can do, too. We can think about who we are and what we would do if we were in the situations described in the stories.*

ACTIVE TIME
Sun and Ice

This game from Mexico, called Sun and Ice, is a team variation of tag. In it, the girls will be moving almost constantly.

Have the Brownies form two teams and decide which team will be the first to try to tag the players on the other team. If a player is tagged, she has to say *ice* and cannot move. She remains frozen until another member of her team tags her and says *sun*. The teams switch roles after five minutes.

Afterward, invite one girl to place a sticky note on Mexico on the globe or world map and say what she enjoyed most about playing Sun and Ice.

A Girl Scout Story

Ask the girls to recall their clue-finding from the last time they got together, and explain that you're going to read a very brief story that not only reveals a clue but shows that everyone, including Juliette "Daisy" Gordon Low, the founder of Girl Scouts, faces challenges in life. Say: *Listen for clues in this true story as I read it. Think about how you'd make a change.* Then read the story:

Daisy was Juliette's nickname. Daisy was born in 1860, just one year before a terrible war broke out in the United States. Some of Daisy's family members were on one side in the war, and some were on the other side. This was hard on everyone.

The war caused another hardship. There wasn't a lot of food in Savannah, Georgia, where Daisy and her family lived. People did not have many of the foods they were used to. For their safety, Daisy and her family went to live with her grandparents in Chicago, Illinois. Even though Chicago was safe and had plenty of food, the long trip and lack of healthy food along the way made Daisy very sick. Her family thought she would die. But Daisy got well!

Her mother believed that Daisy willed herself to get well. She said maybe that was why Daisy—Juliette—was very strong-willed later in her life.

Now get the girls talking about clues and the changes they can suggest. Ask:

- *What was hard for Daisy's family when she was a baby?*
- *What did her family do to make things better?*
- *What would you have changed about Daisy's world to make it better?*
- *Do any of the problems that she faced still exist today? Is there anything we can do about them?*

Closing Ceremony: My Favorite Part

Invite the Brownies to form a circle, close their eyes, and think back to earlier times in the journey. Say something like:

You've learned how stories have clues for change, and you each found your own clue. Then together you chose a change, planned a project, and made it happen. All along the way, you've been learning about your world of girls.

Now ask the girls to open their eyes and tell which parts of the journey they have enjoyed most so far.

Looking Ahead
to Sessions 7 & 8

In the next Session, the girls have an opportunity to begin planning how they will tell others about the change they made in their world. Look back at the "4 Brownie Awards" chart on page 47 to remind yourself of the flow of awards along this journey and how the Brownies will now educate and inspire others about the change they carried out. The girls will do the "telling," so don't plot it out for them! Just be ready to get some ideas going, and have your assistants offer ideas, too. The important thing is for the Brownies to understand how telling others about what they did helps keep the change going, and that by keeping the change going and inviting others to Take Action, too, they're making the world a better place! Get ready to engage girls in this process by asking them to think about who they might be telling the story of their change to.

If you're planning on sharing public service announcements (PSAs) with the girls, look over "Media Stories That Do Good" (page 80), and arrange to have a computer with Internet access available.

Also, ask each girl to look through magazines or newspapers for advertisements that show girls, and to try to bring in one or two. The girls in the ads should be roughly their age or slightly older. Explain to the Brownies that they will be looking at these and other ads to explore how the media tells stories of girls— and to see what media can teach them about inspiring others.

Some girls might not bring in their own advertisements, so make sure you have enough ads on hand for each girl to examine one closely. Look for ads that show girls in a way that implies they are now happier or more popular, or that shows stereotypical views of girls. Reach out to your Network for art supplies so the girls can alter the ads or make new ones.

SAMPLE SESSIONS 7 & 8
Planning and Telling Our Story of Change

WORKING OUT THE DETAILS

Sessions 7 and 8 are set aside as time for the Brownies to focus on what they will do to earn their Tell a Story Award—after they take time to earn their Change a Story Award!

Depending on the time the girls have and the nature of what they are doing, you might schedule an additional gathering for the girls to tell their story. They then earn their Tell a Story Award at the start of Session 9.

The specific activities you and the girls choose for these sessions will depend on the Brownies' interests and their project. These sessions are also a good time to show a DVD or video clips of various ways stories are told in the arts, or a video of a professional storyteller or of someone telling traditional tales from another culture. Ask a librarian to recommend a video.

Other activities offered here can be enjoyed apart from, and along with, the girls' project. So have fun with what you and the Brownies have time for—and save the rest for another day!

AT A GLANCE

Goal: The Brownies gain confidence by planning for and telling an audience the story of the change they made, and inspiring that audience to keep the change going.

- **Opening Ceremony: Earning the Change a Story Award**

- **Ads Among Us**

- **Option: Create Your Own Ads**

- **Planning to Tell Our Story of Change**

- **We Are Like This**

- **Optional Ceremonies**

MATERIALS

- **Opening Ceremony:** Change a Story awards for each Brownie

- **Ads Among Us:** at least one print ad per Brownie (see page 77)

- **Helpful Stories:** public service announcements (PSAs) in print or a computer with Internet access to show online PSAs.

- **Create Your Own Ads** (Option): scissors, glue, paper, drawing materials

- **Planning to Tell Our Story of Change:** any art materials the girls need for telling their story

PREPARE AHEAD

- If possible, invite a Cadette earning her LiA Award to attend this session and lead the girls in "Create Your Own Ads" and in exploring ways to tell their story to a public audience. She could also help with the preparation for the next session's public storytelling.

- Flip through the ads you found and think about the stories behind them.

- If you plan to show PSAs online, preview them and make sure they are appropriate for Brownies. Also, bookmark the Web sites you'll be sharing, so that you can find the announcements easily during the session.

- Make copies of the invitation to the Tell a Story event on page 83.

AS GIRLS ARRIVE

Display the Team Passport. Today's contribution(s) to the Passport might be one or more ads the girls make.

Opening Ceremony: Earning the Change a Story Award

For this Opening Ceremony, invite the girls to stand in a circle. Remind them of the steps they took to earn their Change a Story Award. Say something like:

- The beginning of our story of change was _____.

- The middle of our story was_____.

- The end of our story was _____.

As you give each girl her Change a Story Award, ask her to describe how it felt to do the project and create a change in her own community. Let the girls give themselves a big round of applause! Then sign or stamp each girl's passport!

LARGE GROUP?

If your group is large and you have assistants or a Cadette with you, split into two or more groups for "Ads Among Us" and the "Create Your Own Ads" option. Or create the groups and rove among them, if you are flying solo. Ask the questions suggested, and keep the fun and learning in high gear!

MEDIA STORIES THAT DO GOOD

Take time to let the Brownies know that media doesn't just sell things—it can also do a lot of good.

Explain that public service announcements, called PSAs for short, are advertisements that raise awareness of important issues, including health and safety ones, such as not smoking and always wearing a helmet while bicycling.

You might show the Brownies a few PSAs on values.com, the Web site of Foundation for a Better Life. These short videos promote the values of honesty and helping others, which echo the Girl Scout Law.

GET CREATIVE!

Ads Among Us

Girls' worlds are full of advertising and media, and this activity will get the Brownies thinking about the stories—both real and fictional—that ads tell about girls. Start by spreading out the ads you and the girls have gathered. Invite each girl to take an ad and spend a minute or two reading and thinking about it. Say something like: *Each ad is like a little story. Ads have characters and some kind of action. Tell me the story of the ad you chose.*

After the girls have described the stories, ask: *Why do you think these ads were created?* Guide the girls to understand that the answer is "to sell something." Help them see that the "story" is often that a product will solve a girl's desire or need, or make her happier than she would be if she didn't have it.

To encourage the Brownies to compare the world they know to the world shown in the ads, ask:

- *Do the stories of these ads seem real to you? Do they seem like something you would find in your life?*

- *Which parts of the ads seem to match your life and the lives of girls you know?*

- *Which parts of the ads seem like they don't match your life?*

- *Do you think these parts are just made up? Or are they not real in your life but might be real in the lives of others?*

Encourage the girls to compare these portrayals of girls in ads to ones of girls in stories they know and have shared on this journey.

OPTION: CREATE YOUR OWN ADS

What better way for the Brownies to understand advertisements than to create their own? Provide the girls with markers and paper, or other art supplies, and invite them to make their own ads. They might choose to:

- Re-create or alter one of the ads they looked at (or other ads they know) to make them truer to their own lives.

- Create an ad highlighting what is special about each girl in their group or about the diversity of girls in general.

- Create an ad to encourage others to read a particular story.

- Plan to make ads for the Tell a Story event (see page 82). The girls might create an ad that announces their event or create ads for their call to action, which concludes their storytelling.

When the girls are ready, invite them to show their ads and share what they think works best in one another's ads.

If the girls need some guidance on how to create an ad, let them know all they need are:

- **A few words** that catch people's attention

- **An inviting image** (photo or drawing) that makes viewers of the ad want to know more or join in

The girls can cut images from existing ads or sketch their own images.

(see page 82)

MATERIALS

- scissors
- glue
- paper
- drawing materials

Planning to Tell Our Story of Change

The girls will use what they've learned about stories, ads, and the media to tell others about their Change a Story project. Explain that one way to create a change that "keeps going" is to encourage others to get involved, too. And telling the story of their change also earns them their Tell a Story Award!

START A BROWNIE BRAINSTORM

To get the Brownies thinking together about an audience to tell their story of change to, ask them some questions like these:

- *Who might be especially interested in the change we are creating?*
- *Who do you think would want to get involved in this change, too?*
- *Is there anyone else—family or special friends? A librarian, others?*

Talk with the girls about whether their audience should be a small number of people, such as those who've been involved with or have assisted on the journey. Or perhaps they prefer to reach out to a broader audience, such as a large group of girls their own age.

What matters most is that the Brownies have a chance to inspire others to make the world a better place, too—and to understand that in doing so, they are creating a change that becomes long-lasting.

ZERO IN ON THE DETAILS!

As the girls know by now, there are so many ways to tell stories! Say: *Let's keep our Brownie Brainstorm going and decide the details of who we could tell our story of change to and what we might inspire our audience to do to keep our good change going!*

What the girls choose to do will depend on the time and resources you and the group have, what interests the girls, and who is best to tell in order to keep their change going. For example, if the girls organized a Family Fitness night for their Change a Story project, who might they want to share its success with? If families from the girls' school attended the event, the Brownies might decide to stage their storytelling at a community center so they can tell their story of change to even more families. These families will perhaps be inspired to organize their own fitness events to reach more families and keep the healthy change going.

FIT THE PROJECT INTO YOUR LIVES

Feeling time-challenged? Think about what you and the girls and their families do during the course of a week. What events can the girls piggyback onto so they can tell their story during school, after school, or at regular weekend activities? Finding an already scheduled "event" will eliminate the need for separate planning and provide a ready-made audience!

The girls could tell their story of change at the community center through . . .

- a skit they create

- a song they write and sing

- a mural they paint and unveil and talk about

- an exhibit of photos or drawings

LEAVE TIME FOR CREATIVITY

Allow time in these sessions for the girls to make props or other materials for whatever storytelling method they decide on.

Also give the girls time to create invitations, using the template below or their own design.

We've got a wonderful story
We'd like to share with you—
It's about an important change
We all can make come true!

Date: _____

Time: _____

Place: _____

From: _____

Brownies on *A World of Girls* Journey

We Are Like This

Gather the Brownies in a circle and say something like:

- *Let's pretend to take a photo of our group. How do we look in the photo? Are we dancing together, sitting together, or something else?*

- *Let's each take a turn saying how we look and how we feel in this photo!*

 ## Optional Ceremonies

Consider these ceremonies for the day of the Brownies' big tell:

SHAKE IT OUT!

On their big day, the girls may be a little nervous about their storytelling. Before their guests arrive, encourage them to use up any nervous energy with some stretching, dancing to a little music, or even jumping jacks or running in place.

Next, ask them to gather in a circle and share one word to describe how they feel ("happy," "nervous," "excited," "proud," etc.).

Then ask them to huddle for a team cheer, just like before a big ball game!

SHAKE IT OUT AGAIN!

After the girls tell their story to the audience, bring them back into a circle and ask them to share one word about how they feel now that they've told their story of change. Let them "shake it out" again (dance, jump, wiggle), but this time in celebration for their accomplishments.

Looking Ahead to Session 9

In the next session, the girls turn inward in preparation for earning their Better World for Girls! Award. They'll focus on their strengths, their confidence, and on ways of expressing themselves. Invite the girls to ask a woman in their lives (mother, grandmother, aunt, older sister, teacher, or another close and trusted female) to name one strength she sees in her Brownie. To show what you mean, you might say: *How would a woman in your life complete this sentence: "I like the way you _____."* Fill in possible strengths, such as: don't give up; dance (or sing) your heart out; challenge yourself; ask thoughtful questions; know when to speak up and know when to let things go; take the lead when things sort of slump a little; use your time on your own in creative ways; look out for others; play fair with everybody.

For "A Special Piece of the Whole," call on your Network to prepare a blank "quilt" square for each girl. Aim for 6-to-8-inch squares of fabric or cut paper that can be painted on, and enough squares to create a full square or rectangle when the quilt is assembled. Each square should have a slit inside each corner for tying the girls' pieces together with string. See the Materials list for "A Special Piece of the Whole" and "Our Whole Story" (page 86). Depending on your group, you might arrange a separate quilting session, when the girls and the women they asked "quilt" together!

If you plan to do the "Painting Mixed Feelings" option, suggest that for their next time together the girls wear clothes they can paint in.

TIPS FOR POSITIVE "CRITIQUES"

- Start with "I like . . ." and praise what's working well.

- Smile. When something isn't working, it's not so serious—it can be fun to fix.

- Use questions to suggest changes. Guide the girls to see on their own what could be improved by asking: *What do you think might help pick up the pace a little? What could you say so I know who that character is? Or what that word means?*

- Ask whether the girls think another way, or solution, might work.

- Use humor. Use surprise. Be brief. You don't want to lose the girls' attention or deflate enthusiasm.

- End with a boost: *You're doing great!* And when the adjustment is made, acknowledge it: *Now you've got it!*

Brownies are
filled with pride
and confidence as they
receive their Tell a Story Award.

OUR WHOLE STORY

SAMPLE SESSION 9
Our Whole Story

AT A GLANCE

Goal: The Brownies earn their Tell a Story Award, consider their place in the world of girls, and begin to plan a celebration of all they've learned and accomplished on this journey.

MAKING THE MOST OF THE GIRLS' BOOK

Activities and discussions in this session correspond to the third story, "Story Swapping with Lakti," on page 28 of the *WORLD* side of the girls' book.

- Opening Ceremony: Earning the Tell a Story Award

- A Special Piece of the Whole

- Our Whole Story

- Pass It On (Option: Painting Mixed Feelings)

- Planning a "Better World for Girls!" Celebration

- Creative Spirit

- Closing Ceremony: Friendship Squeeze

MATERIALS

- **Opening Ceremony:** Tell a Story awards for each Brownie

- **A Special Piece of the Whole:** quilt squares or cut paper; markers, crayons, and/or colored pencils; scissors, glue, rulers; assorted art supplies, such as stickers, yarn, felt, cotton balls, ribbon, beads, glitter

- **Our Whole Story:** string or yarn in 6-inch lengths, tape

- **Pass It On:** world map or globe, sticky notes; for **"Painting Mixed Feelings":** paint, paint brushes, paper

Pages 28–29, *WORLD* side of the Brownies' book

PREPARE AHEAD

- Read the profile of Faith Ringgold (girls' book, *GIRLS* side, page 34) and "Story Swapping with Lakti" (starting on page 28, in the *WORLD* side). Review the activities about girls' worlds, such as "Picturing Your World of Girls" on pages 12–13 in the *GIRLS* side.

AS GIRLS ARRIVE

If they haven't done so already, ask the girls to add their contributions to the Team Passport to capture their Tell a Story teamwork from the previous sessions. Chat with assistants about setting up the art materials for the quilt squares and any painting station needed for the optional "Painting Mixed Feelings" activity.

Opening Ceremony:
Earning the Tell a Story Award

Gather the girls together and recall some highlights of how they told their story of change at their last gathering. Then present each girl with her Tell a Story Award. To wrap up, ask the girls to chant the following lines:

A changed story we did tell.
Our excitement never fell!
We inspired people high and low.
Now our change will grow and grow!

Take a few minutes to sign or stamp all the girls' individual passports and remind the girls to complete the Tell a Story Award passport page in their book (page 39 of the *GIRLS* side).

Page 34, *GIRLS* side
of the Brownies' book

A Special Piece of the Whole

Start this creative activity by saying something like:

As you've traveled through A World of Girls, *you've learned the stories of many other girls. Now it's time to think about your own story. All of you asked a woman you know to name one of your strengths. We're now going to get creative with that strength!*

Explain that the girls will create a quilt square that tells the story of one thing they do really well (a strength). Point them to the profile of Faith Ringgold on page 34 of the *GIRLS* side of their book. Let the girls know that Ringgold creates quilts that tell stories. You might ask:

Do you know what a quilt is? (Answer: A quilt is a blanket made of squares of fabric that are pieced together side by side or in special patterns.)

Well, a story quilt is a quilt that tells a story with its colors, pictures, and maybe also words. A story quilt can include a poem, a portrait, photographs, or whatever the artist likes. You are the artist today!

Then give the girls one blank quilt square each, and invite them all to write or draw or glue something on their square to represent the strength seen in them by the women they know. Ask them to be sure to include their name on their square.

After the girls are finished, have them share their squares, so the rest of the girls can guess what strength the square depicts.

Then talk together about their strengths. You might ask:

- *How did it feel when someone guessed your strength correctly?*

- *Were any of you surprised by what some of the strengths were?*

- *What other strengths can you name in one another?*

Our Whole Story

Now, explain to the girls that even though their one square is small, all of their many squares together can tell a big story about their team. Say something like: *The squares you created each tells about a single girl, and when we put them together, we'll have something that tells the story of our Brownie world of girls.*

Invite the girls to lay out the squares in an arrangement they like. Give each girl pieces of string or yarn to tie the corners of her square to the ones adjacent to it. Once tied, tape the backs of the squares together more securely. If possible, hang the quilt and invite the girls to step back and admire their handiwork. You might ask: *What do you like most about seeing all of your strengths together?*

If you don't have time to assemble the quilt fully in this session, number the backs of the squares to reassemble them later. If you chose fabric, consider asking a member of your Network to do any necessary sewing after this session.

Now use the quilt to help the Brownies see how they are part of a wider world of girls—their Brownie group. Ask each girl to take a minute or two to think about her connection to her Brownie group and then to the larger world of girls—all girls in the world.

Then say something like:

- *Keep thinking of all the ways you feel part of a world of girls.*

- *Next time we meet, as you earn your final journey award, you will each make another work of art—about you and your world of girls, how you feel about the world of girls, and what that world means to you.*

- **The word Inuit** means "the people" in the Inuit language of Inuktitut. The Inuit live near the Arctic Circle in northern Canada, Alaska, Greenland, and Siberia. They lived in North America long before Europeans arrived there.

- **The Inuit traditionally traveled** by kayak and dogsled, and wore clothing made of the skins of animals they hunted. Some Inuit lived in igloos made of blocks of ice.

- **In 1999,** the government of Canada created the province of Nunavut for the Inuit. Nunavut, which means "our land," is to the east of the Northwest Territories and to the west of Hudson Bay.

- **Storytelling was** traditionally a way for the Inuit to pass the long, dark winters. Many Inuit stories were about the sun, moon, seas, and animals.

- **One storytelling tradition** is known as storyknives. These are blunt knives that Inuit fathers carved from bone or ivory for their daughters. The girls used the knives to draw pictures in the snow or mud to illustrate the stories they told. Some of the knives have intricate carvings on the handles.

- **The Inuit have** traditionally carved figures from stone, animal tusks, and other materials.

Pass It On

Ask the girls what they remember about the third story in the *WORLD* side of their book (beginning on page 28), in which Alejandra, Jamila, and Campbell meet Lakti in Arctic Canada. If the girls haven't read the story, spend time reading all or part of it now.

Share with the Brownies some of the information about the Inuit people at left. Then ask a Brownie to place a sticky note on northeastern Canada on your world map (or globe), and say one thing she learned about girls there.

Then discuss with the girls the Ungava Inuit tradition of oral storytelling, saying something like:

- *People all over the world pass stories on to one another. Some do so by telling their stories aloud. They might sit in a circle and tell their stories to one another, just as you might sit in a circle around a campfire and tell stories in Girl Scouts.*

- *Some storytellers now record themselves telling stories on video or film. That way they can put their stories on the Internet and reach many more people.*

Ask the girls to form two or three small groups. Invite each group to think of a story, either from a book they've read, a folktale or fairy tale they know, or a movie or television show that the other girls will be familiar with. Have them take turns telling their stories. Encourage them to "ham it up" and tell their story with various voices and gestures.

OPTION: PAINTING MIXED FEELINGS

Get this activity started by saying something like:

- *As we all know, stories have a beginning, a middle, and an end. We might have different feelings associated with each of these. We might feel excited at the beginning of a story. Or we might feel nervous.*

- *Think about your experiences all along this journey.*

- *Think about how you felt at the beginning and how you feel now.*

- *Now let's each make a painting that shows these feelings. Maybe you felt the same all along the way. That's OK. And it's also OK to feel more than one way at the same time.*

- *Just make sure your painting shows your feelings. Let your painting tell the story ot how you felt along our journey.*

When the girls are done, let them choose as a team whether they would like to hang their paintings or share them later at their final celebration.

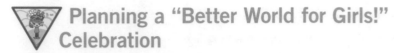

Planning a "Better World for Girls!" Celebration

Invite the girls to plan a party, big or small, to celebrate their journey and the wonderful world of girls. Say something like:

- *It's up to you to decide how to celebrate and who to invite.*

- *You can also decide what foods we'll serve. These can be foods from around the world, or a menu of your own, or your family's favorite foods.*

GO ALL OUT WITH ART

Encourage the girls to think about their interests and talents, and then, together, decide on two or three "creation stations," where they can try out a few art activities in celebration of all they've done along the journey. Call on your Friends and Family Network to gather creative supplies for the stations.

Creative Spirit

Get started by saying something like:

- *As we've traveled on this journey, we've learned a lot about girls near you and far away.*

- *We've thought about what it means to be part of a world of girls.*

- *At our celebration, you'll take the next step and make something creative to show what being part of the world of girls means to you.*

Pages 32–33, *GIRLS* side of the Brownies' book

team talk!

With help from other adults or Cadettes, talk with the girls about the options on hand for materials, based on however many creation stations they would like to set up. To help the Brownies choose a medium (or more than one), refer them to the "Express Your Best" list in their books (page 32–33 of the *GIRLS* side) and ask:

- *Do you like to perform in front of others? Then you might want to write music to play, make up a dance, or shoot a short video of yourself acting.*

- *Do you love words? You could write a little story, a poem, or a song.*

- *Do you like to take photos? Maybe you'd like to put together a photo show.*

- *Do you love to draw or make pictures with lots of color? You could make a painting of a world of girls or create a cartoon.*

- *Do you enjoy putting things together? You could make a book or a collage, or you might sculpt or build something.*

Ask the girls to also think about decorations for their celebration. In addition to any creative projects they make at their final celebration, and their Team Passport, they can display the globe or map they've added to all along the journey, their portraits, quilt, and any ads, posters, or photos from their Change a Story project.

Option: Quilting Bee: If anyone in your Network has a particular talent in quilting, you might want to display the quilt the girls made and place some blank squares and art supplies nearby. After the award presentation, the Brownies could name the strengths they see in their guests, and the guests could create squares that show those strengths. The Brownies might join in and make squares, too.

Option: More World Connections: So that the Brownies see even more ways they are connected to the world, invite families and friends to add sticky notes to countries on the journey globe or world map. On each note, guests can write their names and how they are connected to those countries.

Once their plans are made, ask the girls to make invitations if they are inviting guests. They can use the template on this page or design their own.

BROWNIES AND A WORLD OF GIRLS

We've enjoyed our journey and want to share it with you. And thank you for all your help and inspiration, too!

Join Us to Celebrate Our Journey

Date: _____

Place: _____

Time: _____

From: _____

SET THE DATE!

When the girls have agreed on some of their celebration details, set the date and time, and give them each a copy of the following checklist to fill out. They might also make invitations for any guests they plan to invite, using the template on the previous page or a design of their own.

CELEBRATION PLANNING CHECKLIST

When and where will we celebrate? _____

_____

_____

Who will I invite? _____

_____

_____

_____

What will I bring? _____

_____

_____

What is my job?

☐ set up   ☐ decorate   ☐ serve food   ☐ clean up

Closing Ceremony: Friendship Squeeze

Gather the girls together and invite them to close this time together with a simple friendship squeeze.

Looking Ahead to Session 10

As the Brownies head out, ask them to keep thinking about how it feels to be part of the world of girls and how they might want to express those feelings in a creative way—through photos, drawing, painting, video, dancing, composing, writing, or something else. Let them know that there will be different options to do so at their celebration!

If you and the girls choose to do so, they will spend part of their final celebration creating individual works of art that show their personal connection to the world of girls.

For a full art celebration, aim to invite some guest artists from your community who can set up several creation stations for the girls (see suggestions on page 98) and also assist them with their artwork. Also call on your Network for creative supplies and for setting up the art stations.

SAMPLE SESSION 10
World of Girls Celebration

AT A GLANCE

Goal: The girls create works of art that express what it means to them to belong to a world of girls, as they celebrate their journey and their place in the world.

MAKING THE MOST OF THE GIRLS' BOOK

This final celebration corresponds to pages 36–37 and 40 of the *GIRLS* side of the Brownies' book, where the girls share the story of their journey and their place in the world of girls.

- Opening Ceremony: Follow the Leader
- Introducing . . . Us
- Creation Station Tips
- Sharing Our Stories

- Earning the Better World for Girls! Award
- Celebrate!
- Closing Ceremony: Our Stories Link Us

MATERIALS

- Whatever materials the girls will need for the creation stations or individual projects planned
- **Earning the Better World for Girls! Award:** awards for each Brownie

PREPARE AHEAD

Set up any creation stations or supplies needed and talk with assistants about what they will do during the session.

Opening Ceremony: Follow the Leader

Gather the girls together for a fun version of Follow the Leader. Ask for a girl to volunteer to be the first leader. What the group must do is up to her! Each girl takes a turn at being the leader and performs one simple action (standing on one leg, hopping once, clapping to a beat) that the rest of the group follows.

Introducing . . . Us

As a way to start the celebration and remind everyone that this journey has been about connecting with other girls, invite each Brownie to stand, say hello to the guests, introduce another Brownie to the larger group, and describe something that the two girls share. She might say something like:

Welcome to our celebration of the world of girls. I am Maria. This is Sarah, and we both do gymnastics (or . . . we both love science, or . . . we both read "American Girl" books).

Then the girl who was just introduced does the same for another girl, and names something they share. Continue until all the girls have been introduced.

Creation Station Tips

It's time to start creating! Some stations may be more popular than others, and girls might work at more than one.

- **Writing:** The girls at this station might be writing a story, a poem, a song, a letter, a script, or story. If a girl is writing something that she or others will perform, they might rehearse in a separate location.

- **Photography/Video:** Equipment is located here, but the girls may be moving about shooting. They might plan images and scenes at this station, and then shoot later on their own. Some might need time to print photos for a display or create a computer slide show, or edit or add to their video. (If a second session isn't an option, help the girls plan where and how to print and/or display the photos.) Talk over how they'll e-mail their completed project to one computer, so it can be used on the day of the celebration.

- **Music/Dance:** Locate this center a bit apart from the others. If the girls are creating a dance or singing, or creating new lyrics to an existing song, they may need assistance with the CD player, computer, or MP3 player.

- **Painting/Coloring and 3-D:** Encourage the girls at these stations to sketch out their ideas first (unless they are following the sketch they made last time), and experiment with materials or feel free to depart from their sketch as they go.

Sharing Our Stories

In this part of the celebration, give each girl a chance to have the spotlight. For some girls, this will mean giving a performance. Others will be displaying and describing a finished work of art they've just created. Ask each girl to present her creation and explain how it shows her connection to the world of girls.

Earning the Better World for Girls! Award

Once all the girls have shared their works of art, present each with her Better World for Girls! Award.

Bring the girls together to reflect on all they've done, what they've learned, the ways they've been skillful leaders on their journey—and what they want for themselves and the world of girls going forward. You might ask the girls one or more of these questions:

- *What are you most proud of that you did together on this journey?*

- *What did you do that boosted your confidence in your abilities and all that you can accomplish?*

- *What do you think you'll remember the most?*

- *What things have you learned that you'll take along with you as you move into your Girl Scout future?*

Then ceremoniously sign or stamp all the girls' individual passports—writing a short, encouraging note if time allows.

CELEBRATE!

Bring out the refreshments and invite everyone to mingle and have fun. Play music from around the world for listening or dancing. Ask someone to take photos of the girls' artwork, the decorations, and festivities. A photo of all the Brownies beside their Team Passport (or globe or world map) will make a great memento of the journey.

Closing Ceremony: Our Stories Link Us

Gather the girls together and ask them to take a quiet moment to reflect on how their own work of art shows their connection to other girls. Then ask the Brownies to link arms and take turns going around the circle saying the first line below and then filling in the second sentence about the girl on her right, until each girl has had a turn.

- *We each have stories to tell, and our stories link us together.*

- *I'm linked to [name of the girl to your right] because _____.*

Now, Take Some Time for Yourself

The girls are probably excited about the Girl Scout story they've just completed. What about you? Take a little time to congratulate yourself and celebrate what you've accomplished. You and the girls may never read a story the same way again!

What are some of the many ways you've **Connected** with the Brownies? How has this journey deepened your connection with the stories of girls and the challenges they face?

....
....
....
....

How did your role as a volunteer benefit a world of girls, especially the Brownies and their community? How did you **Take Action** to inspire and foster a sustainable change for the better?

....
....
....
....

What insights have you **Discovered** by exploring stories about girls and women the world over, and by taking action to make their worlds better?

....
....
....
....

A new story begins for you, too. What's next?

....
....
....
....

NATIONAL LEADERSHIP OUTCOMES

Every experience in this Brownie *World of Girls* journey
is designed to help girls be confident leaders
in their daily lives—and in the world!

Discover	**+**	Connect	**+**	Take Action	**=**	Leadership

DISCOVER

Girls understand themselves and their values
and use their knowledge and skills to explore the world.

	AT THE BROWNIE LEVEL, girls . . .	RELATED ACTIVITIES (by Session or girls' book chapter/activity)
Girls develop a strong sense of self.	Positively identify with their gender and cultural, linguistic, racial, and ethnic groups.	S1: Games Around the Globe, Our Globe (or Map) of Girls; S2: Opening Ceremony; The Center of Your World, Overlapping Worlds, Girls in Stories; S3: Sweet, Spicy, Smooth and Bright; S7&8: Ads Among Us, Create Your Own Ads, Closing Ceremony; Take it Home; S9: Opening Ceremony; A Special Piece of the Whole, Our Whole Story, Planning a Better World for Girls Celebration; GB-G: First, Your Passport, Your Brownie World, The World Is Filled With Girls . . . , Picturing Your World of Girls, All Our Stuff Has Stories, Windows on the World, Stories Can Plant Seeds of Understanding, Express Your Best!, Your Place in the World of Girls, My Passport Tells a Great Story, A Better World for Girls Award
	Have increased confidence in their abilities.	All sessions, stories, and activities
Girls develop positive values.	Begin to apply values inherent in the Girl Scout Promise and Law in various contexts.	S1: Opening Ceremony; S3: Two Story Relays; S4: Giving, Sharing, Changing; S7&8: Opening Ceremonies; GB-W: Flying Into Shali's Desert Home, Dancing with Chosita, Story Swapping with Lakti; GB-G: The Trefoil, the Girl Scout Symbol
Girls gain practical life skills—girls practice healthy living.	Are better at making healthy choices and minimizing unhealthy behaviors.	All Active Times; S1: Games Around the Globe, Snack Time: Jordan's Refreshments; S4: Let's Face It...No, Let's Eat It!, Thai Lettuce Wraps; GB-W: Flying Into Shali's Desert Home, Dancing with Chosita, Story Swapping with Lakti; GB-G: Jumping for Clues, Food Can Remind You of a Story . . . , Make Your Own *Bento*
Girls seek challenges in the world.	Are more open to learning or doing new and challenging things.	All art activities; S1: Games Around the Globe, S2: Closing Ceremony; S3: Opening Ceremony; S3: Our Own Bookmobile; S7&8: Create Your Own Ads; S9: Pass it On; GB-W: all A World of Girls fill-in items, GB-G: Stories and Their Clues, Inventions Are Stories That Change Things for the Better, Changing Stories for the Better, So Many Ways to Make Art, Hear a Story Award, Change a Story Award
Girls develop critical thinking.	Are increasingly able to consider other viewpoints in deciding what to do or what to believe.	S1: The Power of Stories; A World of Girls: First Thoughts; S2: Shali's Story: Clues for Change, Finding Clues All Around; S3: Role-Playing Positive Change, Two Story Relays; S4: Giving, Sharing, Changing; S7&8: Ads Among Us, Planning to Tell a Story of Change; S9: Opening Ceremony; GB-W: Flying Into Shali's Desert Home, Dancing with Chosita, Story Swapping with Lakti; GB-G: Parks Make the World Better, Hear a Story Award, Change a Story Award
	Are better able to recognize and examine stereotypes (based on gender, race, income, ability, etc.) that they encounter.	S2: Shali's Story: Clues for Change, Finding Clues All Around; S4: Giving and Sharing; S7&8: Ads Among Us; GB-G: Little Stories All Around You

S=Session, GB-W=Girls' Book, *WORLD* side, GB-G=Girls' Book, *GIRLS* side

CONNECT

Girls care about, inspire, and team with others locally and globally.

	AT THE BROWNIE LEVEL, girls . . .	RELATED ACTIVITIES (by Session or girls' book chapter/activity)
Girls develop healthy relationships.	Begin to understand how their behavior contributes to maintaining healthy relationships.	S3: Role-Playing Postive Change; S4: Giving, Sharing, Changing, Saying How It Feels to Me; S10: Opening Ceremony; GB-W: Flying Into Shali's Desert Home, Dancing with Chosita, Story Swapping with Lakti; GB-G: A Book Lover, Sharing Is a Way to Change Things, Teaming Up, Adele Ann Taylor's Literacy Library
	Are better able to show empathy towards others.	S3: Role-Playing Positive Change; S4: Saying How It Feels to Me; Closing Ceremony
Girls feel connected to their communities, locally and globally.	Have greater interest in participating in community events, activities, and social networks.	S1: Girl Scouts Around the World; S10: Better World for Girls! Award, Closing Ceremony; GB-G: Parks Make the World Better, Changing Stories for the Better, Change a Story Award
	Recognize the importance of being part of a larger community.	S1: Our Globe (or Map) of Girls, Games Around the Globe; S2: Overlapping Worlds, Me and My Girl Worlds; S7&8: Optional Ceremony; S9: A Special Piece of the Whole, Our Whole Story; S10: Better World for Girls! Award, Sharing Our Stories; GB-W: all A World of Girls fill-in items; GB-G: Parks Make the World Better, Changing Stories for the Better, Change a Story Award, Better World for Girls! Award
Girls can resolve conflicts.	Are better able to apply basic strategies for conflict resolution when conflicts arise.	S4: Saying How It Feels to Me
Girls advance diversity in a multicultural world.	Begin to understand the meaning of diversity.	S2: Me and My Girl Worlds, Girl Worlds in Stories; S3: Sweet, Spicy, Smooth, and Bright; S7&8: Optional Ceremonies; S9: Opening Ceremony; A Special Piece of the Whole, Our Whole Story; GB-W: all A World of Girls fill-in items
	Strengthen their appreciation of differences in others.	All Stories, S1: Snack Time: Jordan's Refreshments; S2: Overlapping Worlds, Me and My Girl Worlds, Shali's Story, More Story Clues All Around, Closing Ceremony; S3: Sweet, Spicy, Smooth, and Bright; S4: Giving, Sharing, Changing; S7&8: Optional Ceremonies; S9: A Special Piece of the Whole, Our Whole Story; GB-W: all A World of Girls fill-in items, Windows on the World, Stories Can Plant Seeds of Understanding

NATIONAL LEADERSHIP OUTCOMES

TAKE ACTION
Girls act to make the world a better place.

	AT THE BROWNIE LEVEL, girls . . .	RELATED ACTIVITIES (by Session or girls' book chapter/activity)
Girls can identify community needs.	Develop basic strategies to identify community issues.	S4: Choosing Our Change and Getting Started on It; S7&8: Planning to Tell Our Story of Change; GB-G: Parks Make the World Better, Changing Stories for the Better, Change a Story Award
	Gain a greater understanding of how Take Action Projects might impact their communities.	S4: Choosing Our Change and Getting Started on It; What If . . . ?; Closing Ceremony; S7&8: Planning to Tell a Story of Change
Girls are resourceful problem solvers.	Are better able to develop a basic plan to reach a goal or a solution to a problem.	S3: Role-Playing Positive Change; S4: Choosing Our Change and Getting Started on It; S5&6: Carry It Out!; S9: Planning a Better World for Girls Celebration; GB-G: Changing Stories for the Better, How to Make a Change You Want to See, Change a Story Award
	Are better able to create alternative solutions to problems.	S3: Role-Playing for Positive Change; S4: Choosing Our Change and Getting Started on It; GB-G: Parks Make the World Better, Changing Stories for the Better, Change a Story Award
Girls advocate for themselves and others.	Gain a better understanding of their rights and those of others.	S4: Saying How It Feels to Me
	Learn and begin to apply basic advocacy skills.	S5&6: Carry It Out, S7&8: Earning the Change a Story Award, Planning to Tell Our Story of Change; S9: Earning the Tell a Story Award
Girls educate and inspire others to act.	Are better able to explain their ideas or teach new skills to others.	S3: Our Own Bookmobile; S5&6: Carry It Out; S7&8: Optional Ceremonies, Media Stories That Do Good; Create Your Own Ads, Planning to Tell Our Story of Change; S9: Earning the Tell A Story Award; S10: Sharing Our Stories; GB-G: Changing the World Means Telling a New Story, Tell a Story Award
	Can communicate their reasons for engaging in community service and action.	S4: Choosing Our Change and Getting Started on It; S5&6: Carry It Out; S7&8: Planning to Tell Our Story of Change; S9: Earning the Tell a Story Award; GB-G: Changing the World Means Telling a New Story, Tell a Story Award
Girls feel empowered to make a difference.	Increasingly feel they have important roles and responsibilities in their groups and/or communities.	S1: Closing Ceremony; S2: Opening Ceremony; Me and My Girl Worlds; S7&8: Optional Ceremonies, Planning to Tell Our Story of Change; S9: A Special Piece of the Whole, Our Whole Story, Planning a Better World for Girls Celebration; S10: Earning the Better World for Girls Award, Closing Ceremony; GB-W: all A World of Girls items; GB-G: The World Is Filled with Girls . . . , Parks Make the World Better, Sharing Is a Way to Change Things for the Better, Teaming Up, Changing Stories for the Better, Your Place in the World of Girls, Better World for Girls Award
	Exhibit increased determination to create changes for themselves and others.	S2: Shali's Story: Clues for Change, Finding Clues All Around; S4: Giving, Sharing, Changing; S5&6: Opening Ceremony; S7&8: Earning the Change a Story Award, Create Your Own Ads, Planning to Tell Our Story of Change; S9: Earning the Tell a Story Award; S10: Earning the Better World for Girls! Award, Closing Ceremony; GB-W: all A World of Girls fill-in items; GB-G: The World Is Filled with Girls, Parks Make the World Better, Sharing Is a Way to Change Things for the Better, Teaming Up, Changing Stories for the Better, A Better World for Girls Award